BASEBALL'S BIGGEST BLOOPERS

BASEBALL'S BIGGEST BLOOPERS

The Games That Got Away

BY

DAN GUTMAN

VIKING

VIKING
Published by the Penguin Group
Penguin Books USA Inc., 375 Hudson Street, New York, New York 10014, U.S.A.
Penguin Books Ltd, 27 Wrights Lane, London W8 5TZ, England
Penguin Books Australia Ltd, Ringwood, Victoria, Australia
Penguin Books Canada Ltd, 10 Alcorn Avenue, Toronto, Ontario, Canada M4V 3B2
Penguin Books (N.Z.) Ltd, 182–190 Wairau Road, Auckland 10, New Zealand

Penguin Books Ltd, Registered Offices: Harmondsworth, Middlesex, England

First published in 1993 by Viking, a division of Penguin Books USA Inc.

1   3   5   7   9   10   8   6   4   2

Library of Congress Cataloging-in-Publication Data
Gutman, Dan.
Baseball's biggest bloopers: the games that got away /
by Dan Gutman.   p.   cm.
ISBN 0-670-84603-1
1. Baseball—United States—Miscellanea.   I. Title. GV867.3.G88   1993
796.357'0973—dc20   92-25933   CIP

Photos captioned "NBL" were provided courtesy of
the National Baseball Library, Cooperstown, New York.
Printed in U.S.A.   Set in 11 point Aster

For Lucy

Acknowledgments

Thanks to editor Elizabeth Law,
who bears the burden
of going through life as a Red Sox fan,
and research assistant Brian Kors,
the only 11-year-old in the world
who knows how many guys
George "White Wings" Tebeau
struck out in 1887.*

*One.

Contents

Introduction   i x

PART I
The Four Most Dramatic Mistakes in Baseball History

1. *The Merkle "Bonehead" Play*   2
2. *The Snodgrass Muff*   1 8
3. *The Owen Dropped Third Strike*   3 4
4. *The Buckner Boot*   4 8

PART II
Other Legendary Bloops and Blunders

5. *Heinie Zimmerman's Dash to the Plate*   6 8
6. *Hank Gowdy Steps in It*   7 8
7. *Hack Wilson: Out in the Sun Too Long*   8 8
8. *Umpire Goats*   1 0 0
9. *Herb Washington: Designated Pick-off Victim* 1 1 2
10. *Curt Flood: It Must Be Up There Somewhere* 1 2 2
11. *Lonnie Smith: Faked Out of the World Series* 1 3 2
12. *Babe Herman: Rush Hour on the Basepaths*   1 4 2

Want to Read More About These Stories?   1 5 3

Index   1 5 5

Introduction

THERE ARE LOTS OF WAYS to say a guy *screwed up*.

You could simply say that he made an *error*, of course, or a *mistake*. You could say he *goofed*. He *flubbed it*. He *muffed it*. He *mangled it*. He *messed up*, big time.

You could open up a thesaurus and dig out some more words that get your point across. He committed a *gaffe*, a *lapse*, a *miscue*, a *slipup*. If it was really bad, you could say he pulled a *howler*, a *screamer*, a real *clanger*.

For some reason, the letter *B* works well—*botch*, *boner*, *blooper*, *bloomer*, *blunder*, *bungle*, *bull*.

If you really want to blow away your friends, you could use big words that make you sound smart. "His baserunning is a study in *ineptitude*, wouldn't you agree?" "He suffered an unfortunate *contretemps* while attempting to catch that fly ball, eh, dude?"

But when it comes to baseball, there's one word that describes a bumbler better than all the others.

Goat. He was the *goat*.

Not the animal kind. Goat is short for *scapegoat*— "One who is made to bear the blame for others or to suffer in their place."

In baseball, a goat is a guy who makes a mistake. A *big* mistake. The kind of mistake that costs his team a big game, the pennant, or maybe even the whole *enchilada*—the World Series.

This book is filled with 'em. You're about to read true stories of guys like Fred Snodgrass, who dropped a fly ball in 1912 that people are still talking about. And Bill Buckner, who let an easy grounder dribble through his legs to blow the 1986 World Series for the Red Sox. (Boston fans will still be talking about that one well into the next century.) And poor Fred Merkle, who made a simple mistake when he was a 19-year-old rookie and had to live with the name Bonehead Merkle for the rest of his life.

You'll read about other goats who got picked off, faked out, tripped up, or who made incredibly stupid plays at precisely the worst possible moment.

Believe it or not, there are lessons to be learned from this. The first one, naturally, is DON'T SCREW UP! Who wants to go through life with people calling you Bonehead?

The second lesson is that even the best in the world screw up now and then. *Nobody's perfect. Mistakes are a part of life. We're only human.* The greatest players in the game make mistakes. The President of the United States makes them. You're going to make them. There's nothing you can do about it.

Making a mistake isn't the end of the world, even if

you just blew the play that would have won the World Series. After the men in this book made their colossal clangers, they didn't give up, retire, or go live in a cave somewhere. They shrugged it off and went on with their lives.

After his baseball career was over, Fred Snodgrass became the mayor of a town in California. Bill Buckner played four more years after missing that easy grounder. Before he retired, he had more career hits than any other active player. He became a popular sportscaster. Don Denkinger went right on umpiring after blowing a controversial call in the 1985 World Series. Mickey Owen, who gave up a passed ball to blow it for the Dodgers in 1941, became *The Sporting News*'s top catcher in the majors the next season. Later, he became a county sheriff.

There's another lesson we can all learn from this book—never leave a baseball game until the last out is made in the ninth inning. You never know what might happen on the field while you're on your way home.

So turn the page and check out some of these incredible screwups, errors, mistakes, goofs, flubs, muffs, gaffes, lapses, miscues, slipups, howlers, screamers, clangers, botch jobs, boners, bloopers, bloomers, blunders, bungles, bulls, and inept contretemps.

And be thankful *you* didn't make them.

—*Dan Gutman*

BASEBALL'S BIGGEST BLOOPERS

PART

I

The Four Most Dramatic Mistakes in Baseball History

Merkle Rushes Off Base Line Before Winning Run Is Scored

and Is

CONFUSIC

Chance

mick's R

Crowd

UMPIRE

Singular Oc

Reported

Who

CHAPTER

1

The Merkle "Bonehead" Play

THE DATE: Thursday, September 23, 1908.
THE PLACE: The Polo Grounds,
New York City.
THE SITUATION: The New York Giants
versus the Chicago Cubs. Bottom of the
ninth, two outs, runner on first.

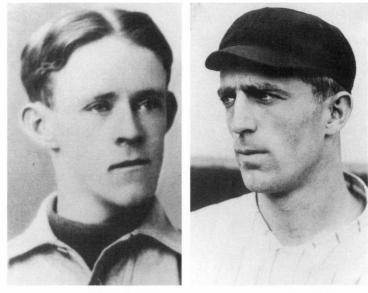

▲ *Johnny Evers (NBL)*   ▲ *Fred Merkle (NBL)*

residen

Score

G

UBS N

anager

Field for

Umpires

According
ulliam of
rs of Mer
een New
e Giants t
pported L
clared th
er of the
contest
ries which
ounds res
o games

The er
not yet
served
he will

According
Pulliam of t
ers of Merk
ween New
he Giants th
upported U
eclared the
her of the
le contest w
eries which

Censurable stupidity on the part of
ayer Merkle in yesterday's game at the
olo Grounds between the Giants and

New York Giants shortstop Al Bridwell. He slapped the single to right center-field that caused his teammate Fred Merkle to be known as "Bonehead" for the rest of his life. (NBL)

*F*REDERICK CHARLES MERKLE stepped up to the plate for the Giants. He was just 19 years old, a rookie first baseman from Watertown, Wisconsin, playing in his first major league game as a starter.

Fred Tenney, the regular first baseman, had awoken that morning with a bad back and sore leg. It was the only game he would miss all season.

Little did Merkle, Tenney, or anyone else realize that this would be one of the most famous and controversial baseball games ever played.

The Giants, managed by the immortal John McGraw, were having a great season. It was a hot and heavy pennant race between the Giants, the Pittsburgh Pirates, and the Chicago Cubs. The Cubs had just come into New York and swept a doubleheader, moving them within one game of the Giants in the standings. The third game of the series was crucial. The Giants couldn't allow themselves to be swept by the team directly behind them. There were less than three weeks left in the season.

One of the greatest pitchers ever, Christy Mathewson, was on the mound for the Giants that day. Jack Pfiester was starting for the Cubs. Pfiester was a mediocre pitcher (12–10 in 1908), but was dubbed Jack the Giant Killer because he had a strange mastery over the New York Giants hitters.

The game was shaping up as a pitchers' duel, since neither team was able to push across a run in the first four innings. In the top of the fifth, shortstop Joe Tinker hit an inside-the-park home run to put the Cubs on the scoreboard.

An inning later, the Giants tied it up. Second baseman Buck Herzog singled and took second base when Cubs third baseman Harry Steinfeldt bobbled the relay. Giants catcher Roger Bresnahan followed with a perfect bunt, and Herzog scampered to third. When right fielder Mike Donlin singled, Herzog jogged home. The score was 1–1. Nobody scored in the seventh or eighth innings.

The bottom of the ninth inning is perhaps the most talked about and unusual inning in more than one hundred years of major league baseball. Here's what happened . . .

THE CUBS DIDN'T SCORE in the top of the ninth. In the bottom of the ninth, center fielder Cy Seymour led off for the Giants. He hit a wicked grass cutter to the right side of the infield, but second baseman Johnny Evers scooped it up and threw him out at first. One out.

Next up was Art Devlin, the Giants third baseman. He took a Pfiester pitch and lined a single to center. The winning run was on first.

Left fielder Moose McCormick stepped up to the plate. McCormick was a left-handed hitter, and he tried to pull the ball to the right side to advance the runner into scoring position. He succeeded in pulling the ball to the right, but once again Johnny Evers plucked the grounder cleanly at second base. Evers flipped to Joe Tinker as Devlin was sliding in. The throw was just in time, and Devlin was a force-out victim. McCormick was safe at first. Two outs.

The Giants had to get something going quickly, or the game would go into extra innings. The sky was starting to darken, and there were no lights or night games in those days.

The next batter was Fred Merkle. He was a big man six feet, one inch tall and 190 pounds. A base hit would advance McCormick to third. A double or better would probably win the game and Merkle—a rookie—would be the hero. He had yet to step up to the plate forty times all year or make his tenth big league hit.

"If he will only single," wrote *The New York Times* the next day, "we will ignore any errors he may make in the rest of his natural life."

Merkle *did* single—a shot down the right-field line. The ball was fair by less than a foot and could have gone for a double, but the Giants were playing cautiously.

They didn't want the winning run to get cut down at the plate.

Okay, here's where it stood: The score was 1–1. Bottom of the ninth. Two outs. McCormick—the potential winning run—was on third. Fred Merkle was on first.

Out of the Giants dugout stepped shortstop Al Bridwell. Everyone in the Polo Grounds knew it was an important moment. Few suspected it was so important that people would remember it more than eighty years later.

Pfiester served up a waist-high fastball right over the plate, and Bridwell slapped a line drive into right center-field. The ball just about hit umpire Bob Emslie, but he dove out of the way. The crowd rose to its feet, roaring. Moose McCormick trotted down the line and stepped on home plate with the apparent game-winning run. Fans poured onto the field, as was the custom in those days.

The New York Giants had won the game. Or so everyone thought.

FREEZE THIS MOMENT. What happened next will probably be debated for centuries. When he saw the ball being hit, Fred Merkle ran off the first base bag toward second. As soon as he saw the ball land in the outfield, he stopped. The game was over, he reasoned, when

McCormick crossed the plate. There was no need to keep running to second base.

Merkle veered off the baseline and headed for the Giants clubhouse, which was behind the bleachers in right center-field. It was a mistake he would regret for the rest of his life.

Merkle wasn't the only one to call it a day. In fact, everybody in the ballpark assumed the game was over except for one man—Chicago Cubs second baseman Johnny Evers.

Evers was one of the shrewdest men ever to play in the majors. He spent his spare time reading *The Official Baseball Rules*, and it paid off because of situations just like this one.

The rules of baseball state very clearly that "if a runner is forced out at any base for the third out in an inning, a run that scores on the play does not count, even if it scored before the force was made."

Merkle was on first base when the ball was hit. If he didn't touch second, the Cubs could simply throw the ball in and tag second, forcing him out. The inning would be over and McCormick's run wouldn't count.

Just three weeks earlier, Johnny Evers had encountered the exact same situation in a game against Pittsburgh. The Pittsburgh runner, assuming the game was over when his teammate crossed home plate, didn't continue on to second base. The Cubs tossed the ball to Evers, who stepped on the bag and claimed that the run didn't count.

The umpire in that game—Hank O'Day—ruled against Evers and the Cubs. O'Day realized afterward, however, that Evers was *right*. Going strictly by the rules, a runner on first who dashes off the field without touching second can still be forced out. The rule had never been enforced, and nobody thought to make an issue of it until Johnny Evers came along.

Hank O'Day, as fate would have it, was the plate umpire when Fred Merkle went running off to the clubhouse.

"THROW ME THE BALL!" screamed Evers to center fielder Solly Hofman. "Throw me the ball!"

Hofman picked up the ball in right center-field and threw it to Evers, but it sailed over his head and bounced toward first base. The crowd was swarming all over the field by that time, and the ball was still in play!

Chicago shortstop Joe Tinker picked up the ball, but New York Giants pitcher Iron Man Joe McGinnity, who had been coaching third base that day, wrestled it away from him.

McGinnity started walking off the field with the ball, but Tinker and two other Cubs climbed on his back and jumped all over him trying to get the ball. McGinnity realized he was overpowered, so he reared back and heaved the ball as far as he could toward the left-field stands.

By that time, Fred Merkle finally realized his mistake. Christy Mathewson and several other Giants hustled him back on the field so he could go touch second base. Several Chicago fans leaped on Merkle, trying to stop him.

It looked like a football game out there. The Polo Grounds was in pandemonium.

Suddenly, a baseball landed near the shortstop position. Maybe it was the game ball, and maybe it was a ball somebody on the Cubs bench had tossed into the fracas. We'll never know for sure.

In any case, a middle-aged fan wearing a bowler hat was the first to see the ball. He picked it up as if it was a souvenir and began walking off the field with it. Floyd Kroh, a left-handed pitcher for the Cubs, asked the man for the ball. The man refused, so Kroh punched him and took it.

Kroh tossed the ball to Tinker, who relayed it to Evers, who stepped on second base and held the ball in the air proudly. It may not have been the most well executed force play ever, but Fred Merkle was—according to the rules—out at second.

The only problem was, the two umpires were already on their way to their dressing room, which was behind home plate. Even *they* thought the game was over when McCormick crossed home plate.

The Cubs, led by Johnny Evers, charged over to the umpires to demand that they call Merkle out and clear the field so the game could continue into the tenth inning.

The scene at the Polo Grounds after the game. The crowd rushed onto the field while the ball was still in play, and players were tackling and punching each other to get the ball. (Brown Brothers)

Umpire Bob Emslie, who dove out of the way to avoid being hit by Bridwell's single, said he hadn't seen the play at second base. The other umpire, Hank O'Day, hadn't seen it either and refused to call Merkle safe or out.

O'Day *did* make one decision though—he proclaimed the game was over on account of *darkness*. Stadium security guards helped the umpires get off the field safely and away from the Cubs, the Giants, and their screaming fans.

Most of the crowd (and players, for that matter) went home thinking the Giants had won the game. At ten o'clock that night, Hank O'Day finally made his call—Merkle had failed to touch second base, so he was out and McCormick's run didn't count. The game ended with a 1–1 tie.

John McGraw and the Giants blew their tops. They felt—with good reason—that they had won fair and square. Hundreds of ball games had ended with players running off the field right after the winning run had scored, and nobody had ever suggested using a loophole in the rules to nullify the run. Christy Mathewson said that if the decision went against the Giants, he would never play professional baseball again.

The Giants issued a formal protest to National League President Harry Pulliam, who spent a week mulling it over. Finally, Pulliam decided to back up his umpire's decision. Merkle was *still* out. The game was *still* tied at 1–1. Pulliam announced that in the unlikely event the Giants and Cubs finished the season in a tie for first place, the two teams would play a one-game playoff to determine the winner of the National League pennant.

NATURALLY, the Giants and the Cubs finished the season in a dead heat—each team with 98 wins and 55 losses. One game would decide the pennant.

Forty thousand people—the largest crowd in the history of baseball up until that point—came to the Polo Grounds on October 8 for the playoff. Again, Mathewson and Pfiester dueled on the mound. This time the Cubs won the game cleanly by a score of 4–2, winning their third straight pennant.

In the record books for 1908, it simply indicates . . .

Chicago: Won 99   Lost 55   Pct. .643
New York: Won 98   Lost 56   Pct. .636

Now you know the full story. The Cubs would go on to win the World Series, beating Detroit four games to one. It was the second straight World Championship for Chicago. More than eighty years have passed since then, and the Cubs have yet to win another one.

What Happened Afterward

POOR FRED MERKLE. The failure of the Giants to win the pennant was blamed entirely on him. The newspapers raked him over the coals.

"All our boys did rather well," reported *The New York Herald*, "if Fred Merkle could gather the idea into his noodle that baseball custom does not permit a runner to take a shower and some light lunch in the clubhouse on the way to second."

When Merkle was pulled out of the lineup the next day and the injured Fred Tenney returned to play first base, *The New York Evening Mail* applauded, "A one-legged man with a noodle is better than a bonehead."

From that moment on, for the rest of his career and the rest of his life, Fred Merkle was known as Bonehead. Anytime he reached first base, people would shout, "Hey, Bonehead, don't forget to touch second!" Merkle became the butt of jokes on the vaudeville circuit. "To merkle" became a part of the English language. When people wanted to say that somebody hadn't shown up for something, they would say he or she "merkled."

It's not really fair to say that Fred Merkle's mental error cost the New York Giants the 1908 pennant. First of all, it was common practice in those days to run right off the field after the winning run had scored. Secondly, the Giants lost 55 *other* games that season, and Merkle had nothing to do with them.

Furthermore, the Giants lost six more games *after* "the Merkle game." If they had won just one of those games, the pennant would have been theirs. And if Merkle had simply struck out instead of getting a hit in the *first* place, he never would have had the chance to make his mistake of a lifetime.

New York Giants manager John McGraw never blamed Merkle for blowing the pennant. (In fact, he made sure Merkle received a raise in salary the following year.) McGraw blamed the umpires and National League President Harry Pulliam.

"I won eleven pennants," McGraw would say years later. "Ten are in the book, but the eleventh was stolen from me in a National League meeting room."

Thirty years after the Merkle game, Hall of Fame umpire Bill Klem agreed with McGraw. It was the umpires and league officials who were the *real* boneheads. Klem said calling Merkle out was "the worst decision in the history of baseball."

DESPITE EVERYTHING HE WENT THROUGH, Fred Merkle had a productive 16-year career in the majors. He helped the Giants win three consecutive pennants in

1911, 1912, and 1913. After he left baseball in 1927, he didn't attend a game for 23 years.

When he returned to the Polo Grounds for an old-timers' game in 1950, Fred Merkle received a round of applause from the crowd. After 42 years, he had finally been forgiven for his "bonehead" play.

Or maybe people just finally forgot about it.

Merkle passed away six years later.

Lifetime Statistics

FRED MERKLE: Years 16, games 1,637, batting average .273, fielding average .985, home runs 61, stolen bases 271.

Did You Know . . .

◆ The Polo Grounds, where this game was played, had perhaps the oddest dimensions of any major league park. It was 260 feet down the foul lines, and the center-field fence was nearly five hundred feet from home plate.

◆ Fred Merkle was an excellent chess player.

◆ Merkle played in just seven games during his last season, but he hit .385 in them.

◆ Merkle played in five World Series for three teams, but his team lost every time.

◆ Six Hall of Famers participated in this game:

Mathewson, Bresnahan, Tinker, Evers, McGraw, and McGinnity.

♦ One time, Merkle hit a home run and a double in one inning. Another time, he hit a double and a triple in a single inning.

♦ Along with eight others, Merkle shares the record for most RBIs in one inning—6.

♦ Merkle stole home 11 times in his career. That puts him twenty-second on the all-time list.

Also in 1908 . . .

♦ The New York Giants paid the astonishing price of $11,000 for minor league pitcher Rube Marquard. He would go on to become a Hall of Famer.

♦ George Baird of Chicago invented the electric scoreboard.

♦ Ed Walsh of the Chicago White Sox won 40 games.

♦ Cleveland's Addie Joss pitched a perfect game.

♦ The song "Take Me Out to the Ball Game" was first introduced to the public.

♦ Umpires became responsible for the game's baseballs. Before this, the home-team manager did the job, and doctored balls would appear on the field when the home team needed a big out.

CHAPTER
2

The Snodgrass Muff

THE DATE: Wednesday, October 16, 1912.
THE PLACE: Fenway Park, Boston.
THE SITUATION: Game 7 of the World
Series between the New York Giants and
the Boston Red Sox. Bottom of
the tenth inning, nobody out.

Fred Snodgrass (NBL)

Snodgrass on the defense.
He would live with his error for 62 years. (NBL)

*7*HE BASEBALL HOVERS IN THE AIR like a helicopter. Sometimes it's hard to judge how far it's been hit, especially when it comes off the bat right at you. It's just hanging in the air. It's coming down. You put your glove up. The bright sun may be competing for your attention. There are lots of people yelling, half of them shouting encouragement, the other half pleading for you to choke, to take your eye off the ball for a millisecond, to drop it.

The ball hits your glove and plops out, hitting the ground with a dull thud that says you messed up.

No time to feel sorry for yourself. Runners are sprinting around the bases, and your teammates are screaming their heads off for you to throw in the ball. After the play is over, you'll have plenty of time to think about what you did wrong.

In some cases, a lifetime.

ON APRIL 5, 1974, an old man named Fred Snodgrass passed away in Ventura, California—the same town in which he was born. The headline above his obituary in *The New York Times* read:

Fred Snodgrass, 86, Dead;
Ball Player Muffed 1912 Fly

Here was a guy who made an error in a baseball game 62 years earlier. It was so memorable that when it came time to sum up the man's life, he was remembered for having once dropped a fly ball.

And you wonder why they say major league ballplayers are under so much pressure!

Fred Snodgrass, or Snow, as he was called, made it to the majors in 1908. That was the year Fred Merkle made his memorable bonehead play that cost John McGraw and the New York Giants the National League pennant. By 1912, Snodgrass was McGraw's regular center fielder. He was 24 years old. Merkle was still around, playing first base for the team.

Snodgrass was known for being a superb defensive outfielder. He was a good hitter, too, but never a power hitter. In 946 big league games, he swatted only 11 home runs.

The Giants were in first place by May 15 and never gave it up. They topped the National League by ten games, winning 103 games and hitting an impressive .286 as a team. The pitching staff featured two future Hall of Famers—Rube Marquard and Christy Mathewson. Marquard had won an amazing 19 games in a row during the regular season. Matty, nearing the end of his career, still won 23.

The Red Sox were tough to beat, too, with Tris

Speaker, Harry Hooper, and Duffy Lewis in the outfield and Smokey Joe Wood on the mound. Wood had won 34 games that year and lost just five, with an ERA of 1.91. Speaker hit .383 to lead the American League.

Still, baseball people in the know thought the Giants looked like a sure thing to demolish the Red Sox in the World Series.

It was almost the other way around. Boston won Games 1, 3, and 4, and looked like they were on their way to a devastating upset. Then the Giants stormed back to tie it up at three games each. The Series would come down to one final game. The winners of that game would be the champions of the world, and the losers would go home and have all winter to wonder what they did wrong.

It was a cold, bleak day in Boston. Fenway Park had just opened that season. The Red Sox management gave out rattles to every fan entering the ballpark. When the rattles were banged against the seats, they made a tremendous racket. Giants manager John McGraw called on his ace, Christy Mathewson, to bring the championship to the Giants for the first time since 1905.

IN THE GIANTS HALF of the third inning, Josh Devore walked on four pitches. Red Murray followed with a long drive to left center. Boston's legendary center fielder,

Tris Speaker, took off for the ball and managed to touch it with the tip of his glove, but it trickled off and rolled all the way to the wall. Devore came around to score and the Giants took a 1–0 lead.

In the sixth inning, the Giants almost got another run. Larry Doyle hit a deep drive to right center. It looked like a home run all the way, but Harry Hooper streaked over, threw himself backward over a low railing and reached up to catch the ball in his bare hand while he was lying on top of the fans in the front row of the bleachers. He crawled out of the stands holding the ball up and the umpires called the batter out. Some people say it was the greatest catch in World Series history.

After he tumbled out of the stands, the Giants complained that it was an illegal catch because Hooper wasn't even on the field when he nabbed the ball. But the umpires let the out stand, at least partially because Hooper had made such a terrific play.

The score remained at 1–0 until the seventh inning, when the roof started falling in on the Giants. It was as though they had suddenly forgotten how to catch a baseball.

With one out, Jake Stahl, who managed and played first base for the Red Sox, lifted a pop fly into short left center-field. Three Giants converged on the ball—shortstop Arthur Fletcher, left fielder Red Murray, and center fielder Fred Snodgrass.

But somehow, incredibly, nobody got it. The ball dropped, like a dead bird, and Stahl was standing on second base. Next, Heinie Wagner walked on four pitches. Men on first and second, nobody out.

The Sox sent up rookie Olaf Henriksen, who had hit .321 during the regular season, to pinch-hit for the pitcher. He swung at Mathewson's first pitch and missed for strike one. Matty buzzed another one over the plate for a called strike two. With a two-strike advantage, Mathewson tried to nip at the corners and tempt the rookie to swing at two pitches out of the strike zone, but Henriksen wouldn't take the bait. The count was 2–2.

Next, Matty threw his famous "fadeaway" pitch. Today we call it a screwball. Henriksen didn't care *what* the pitch was called—he ripped it down the left-field line. The ball nicked the third-base bag and rolled into foul territory. Stahl came around from second base to score. The game was now tied at 1–1, and the Fenway Park rattles were deafening.

That's the way it stayed through the eighth and ninth innings. Smokey Joe Wood was on the mound for the Sox by that time. Wood was one of the fastest pitchers ever. He had already beaten the Giants in Game 1 and Game 4, and his fastball was burning holes in the air.

It was going to be Wood against Mathewson for the championship of the world, in extra innings.

Top of the tenth. One out. Giants up. Red Murray slammed a ball into the left-field gap for a two-bagger—his second of the day. Up to the plate strode first baseman Fred Merkle—the same Fred Merkle who made the historic "bonehead" play that crushed the hopes of the Giants four years earlier. If Merkle could get a hit here and drive in the runner at second, maybe people would forget that he blew the season for the Giants in 1908.

Merkle came through, punching a single to center. Murray took off with the crack of the bat. As he rounded third, Tris Speaker got to the bouncing ball. It looked like there would be a close play at the plate. But Speaker, in his haste to pick up the ball, bobbled it. Murray came around to score easily. Giants 2, Red Sox 1.

Wood ended the inning by stopping a line drive off the bat of Chief Meyers with his pitching hand and throwing him out at first. Wood's hand swelled up, and he was done for the day.

Now the Giants needed just three outs to be the World Champions, and Fred Merkle would be the hero. They had the best pitcher in baseball on the mound. How could they lose?

"Is Mathewson apprehensive as he walks to the box?" reported *The New York Times* the next day. "He is not. All the confidence that was his when the blood of youth ran strong in his supple muscles is his now."

The Red Sox sent up Clyde Engle to pinch-hit for Smokey Joe Wood. Engle was a reserve who had only played in 57 games all season and hit only .234.

FREEZE THIS MOMENT. The next pitch is one that many people—especially Fred Snodgrass—would remember for decades. Mathewson reared back and fired the ball. Engle swung and lifted a lazy fly ball to center. One writer described it as a "cupcake."

The baseball expression *a can of corn* isn't used much anymore. Fans used to describe routine fly balls as "a can of corn" because catching one was as easy as grabbing a toppling can from a grocery store shelf. The ball hit toward Snodgrass was a typical can of corn that any high-school player could catch.

Snodgrass was positioned perfectly. He only needed to drift about ten feet to his right and back a few steps.

There was no videotape in 1912, so we'll never know exactly what happened. The newspapers of the day reported that the ball trickled through Snodgrass's glove and the crowd let out a gasp. When the dust had settled, Engle was sitting pretty on second base, and the crowd was going crazy.

"He hit a great big, lazy, high fly ball halfway between Red Murray in left field and me," Snodgrass told baseball historian Lawrence Ritter years later. "Murray called for it first, but as center fielder I had preference over left and right, so there'd never be a collision. I yelled that I'd take it and waved Murray off, and—well—I dropped the darn thing."

CHRISTY MATHEWSON was stunned. In the seventh, three of his teammates failed to catch a simple fly ball. Now, with the whole season on the line, Snodgrass blows one. If Matty was going to win this game, he was going to have to fight for it. There were still no outs.

Harry Hooper stepped up to the plate for Boston. It was an obvious bunting situation. If Hooper could move the runner to third, it would be easy to bring him home and tie the game on a single or a fly ball.

The Giants infield and outfield moved in so they could try to nail Engle at third. Hooper bunted the first pitch, but the ball rolled foul. The bunt sign was taken off for the next pitch. Hooper took a full cut and hit a long drive to deep center. It looked like it could go for three bases. Snodgrass was playing shallow, so as soon as the bat hit the ball, he turned his back and ran as quickly as he could. He caught up with the ball near the warning track and made a spectacular over-the-shoulder catch. He whipped the ball back to second, and Engle made a mad dash to get back to the bag just before the tag. One out. Two to go.

"Snodgrass ran like the wind," Hooper said, "and dang if he didn't catch it. I think he outran the ball. Robbed me of a sure triple."

Christy Mathewson appeared to be rattled by the last two batters. He walked second baseman Steve Yerkes, a .252 hitter. Men on first and second, one out. If nothing else, walking Yerkes set up a force play at any base and would make it easier for the Giants to complete a World Series–ending double play.

Tris Speaker stepped up to the plate. To stay out of a double play, he knew he had to keep the ball off the ground. Mathewson wound up and threw a slow fade-away. It fooled Speaker, but he got the bat on the ball and lofted a high foul pop-up between home plate and first base. This would make two outs and put Boston's backs to the wall.

Fred Merkle, playing first base, came in for the ball. Chief Meyers, the catcher, came out. Mathewson came running off the pitcher's mound. Any of them could have caught the ball easily.

But nobody did. Meyers made a last-second dive for

the ball, but just missed it. Incredibly, for the second time, three Giants had converged on an easy pop-up, and not one of them touched the ball.

By now, even the soft-spoken Christy Mathewson had reached his breaking point. The newspapers reported that he was making angry gestures as he walked slowly back to the mound. A pitcher can only do so much to win a game. He can't strike out every hitter. The defense around him has to do its part.

Shaking his head with relief and amazement, Tris Speaker stepped back into the batter's box.

"That's gonna cost you the ball game!" Speaker shouted to Mathewson.

He had been given a life, and he was determined to take advantage of it. On Matty's next pitch, Speaker lined a screaming single into right field. Engle came in to score the tying run easily. Yerkes stopped at third, and Speaker took second base on the throw home.

Now there were runners on second and third. The run that would win the World Series for Boston was 90 feet from home plate. A wild pitch, a passed ball, a hit, error, or even a fly ball would bring the run in.

McGraw, undoubtedly steaming in the dugout, instructed Mathewson to walk Duffy Lewis intentionally to load the bases. The Giants' only hope was for Matty to strike out the next hitter—Larry Gardner—or get him to hit the ball on the ground for a double play.

Clearly, it wasn't the Giants' day. Matty got the ball up a bit too high and Gardner sent a fly ball to right. Josh Devore caught it and made a desperate throw for the plate, but it wasn't even close. Yerkes tagged up from third, and trotted across the plate.

The Red Sox were the World Champions. Matty and the Giants walked glumly off the field. Fenway Park was in a frenzy.

"Never since that memorable night when Kid Revere rode to Lexington and started the tenth inning rally has Boston been so worked up," wrote sportswriter Hugh Fullerton, "for the Red Sox are champions of the world by virtue of a victory due more to sheer luck than anything else, and tonight the Tories from New York are fleeing homeward beaten in the toughest luck finish that ever was known in a series of this sort."

What Happened Afterward

WITH THE FINAL PLAY, grown men were openly weeping. Wilbert Robinson, John McGraw's right-hand man and former teammate, collapsed in the Giants dugout. Sportswriter Fred Lieb, who accompanied the Giants on their train home, said that Snodgrass "sat like a man in a trance, his eyes glued to the window."

The New York Times started their report on the game with the words: "Write in the pages of World's Series history the name of Snodgrass. Write it large and black. Not as a hero; truly not. Put him rather with Merkle, who was in such a hurry that he gave away a National League championship."

The difference between the winning and losing team's share of the World Series gate was $30,000, and the Snodgrass error came to be known as "the $30,000 muff."

LIKE THE MERKLE DISASTER, Snodgrass didn't deserve his fate. Yes, he was responsible for putting the tying run on base. But his teammates—Mathewson, Merkle, Meyers, and others—had *all* made mistakes and played a part in blowing a sure-thing victory. The Giants committed a whopping 17 errors in the World Series, five of them in Game 2 alone.

So here it was, four years after Fred Merkle's "bonehead" play, and *another* Fred gets the rap for losing a championship for the New York Giants.

But McGraw didn't blame Fred Merkle for his mistake, and he never blamed Fred Snodgrass for *his*.

"Snodgrass didn't lose that game," McGraw said. "The game was lost when Speaker's foul wasn't caught."

It was Snodgrass, unfortunately, whom history remembered.

Lifetime Statistics

FRED SNODGRASS: Years 9, games 946, batting average .275, fielding average .967, home runs 11, stolen bases 215.

Did You Know . . .

◆ Fred Snodgrass hit 20 or more doubles five times.

◆ Three times during his career, Snodgrass got the only hit for his team and broke up no-hitters.

◆ Snodgrass hit .321 in his rookie season, making him the first National League rookie to hit .300 or better. Only eight others have done it since, and none since 1940.

◆ After this World Series, the Red Sox won the Series three times in four years—1915, 1916, and 1918. They have not won since.

◆ Before he joined the New York Giants, Christy Mathewson was the class president at Bucknell University and a member of the glee club and literary society. He played a big part in making baseball a respectable profession for young men. Mathewson would go on to win 373 games and 80 shutouts in his 17-year Hall of Fame career.

◆ Mathewson's younger brother Henry was also a major league pitcher—he pitched three games for the New York Giants in 1906–7. Henry's career totals are:

11 innings, 14 walks, 8 hits, 2 strikeouts, no wins, 1 loss, and 2 saves.

◆ The career of Boston center fielder Tris Speaker spanned nearly the same years as Ty Cobb's, and Speaker played in Cobb's shadow for two decades. His lifetime batting average was .344 (Cobb hit .367), and Speaker had more doubles (792) than any man who ever played the game. He was elected to the Hall of Fame in 1937.

Also in 1912 . . .

◆ Rube Marquard won 19 straight games for the New York Giants.

◆ Brothers Homer and Tommy Thompson were catcher and pitcher for the Yankees, the only time in baseball history that brothers formed a battery. Homer played one major league game as catcher and got no hits. Tommy pitched in seven games, and didn't win any of them.

◆ Tiger Stadium opened.

Yanks Are
Jubilant In
Clubh

FANS SIT ST

Cons

For

th

Tommy
For Ow
Mates W
ter Pulli

Breath
the M
Aga

CHAPTER
3

The Owen
Dropped Third Strike

THE DATE: Sunday, October 5, 1941.
THE PLACE: Ebbets Field, Brooklyn,
New York.
THE SITUATION: Game 4 of the World
Series between the Brooklyn Dodgers and
the New York Yankees. Bottom of
the ninth inning, Dodgers leading 4–3.
Two outs. Full count.

Mickey Owen (NBL)

NNED AFTER DEBACLE

nation Follows Shift in
es—One Asks, 'Are
ums Really Bums?'

*Owen
Shoulde*

The umpire signaled strike three and the game should have been over, but the ball squirted away from Owen, and Tommy Henrich raced for first. He made it safely, and the Yankees came back to bury the Dodgers. (AP/Wide World Photos)

he ball hit
, got away
ime I got
ner of the
ouldn't have
at

Yanks Could 'Catch Lightning
In a Bottle,' Durocher
Remarks After Game

Tommy Henrich Sorr
For Owen But Rest
Mates Whoop It Up A
ter Pulling Out Victor

*T*HOUSANDS OF MAJOR LEAGUE GAMES have been won when a team came from behind in the bottom of the ninth inning. Many times a team has been down to its last out and come back to win the game. Every so often, a team will be down to its last *strike* and come back to win (see "The Buckner Boot," Chapter 4).

It may sound hard to believe, but the 1941 New York Yankees came back to win Game 4 of the World Series *after the game was over!*

It was all due to a regrettable play by Brooklyn Dodgers catcher Mickey Owen, a play he would be remembered by for the rest of his life. The article on the front page of *The New York Times* the next day called Owen's play "one of those harrowing events that doubtless will live through all the ages of baseball like the Fred Snodgrass muff and the failure of Fred Merkle to touch second."

Here's what happened . . .

BROOKLYN DODGERS FANS affectionately called their team "the Bums" in those days. Brooklyn usually fielded a strong team, but it had never won a World Series, and the fans had grown accustomed to their annual battle cry—"Wait till next year."

In 1941, the Dodgers managed to win 100 games for the first time in the team's history and squeaked by the

St. Louis Cardinals to win the National League pennant by two and a half games. For the first time in 21 years, the Brooklyn Dodgers were in the World Series.

In the American League, the powerhouse Yankees cruised to the pennant by 17 games. This was the year Joe DiMaggio hit in an astonishing 56 consecutive games. (It's still the record, more than fifty years later.)

Because both teams were from New York City, the World Series was called a "subway series"—the first of seven the Yanks and Dodgers would battle in over the next 15 years. The Yankees were heavy favorites, which made Brooklyn the sentimental favorite with fans. "Moider duh Yanks!" the Dodgers' always-hopeful fans screamed.

The Yankees won two of the first three games, so Game 4 was a "must" win for the Dodgers. If they could win the game, the Series would be all tied up at two games each. If they lost, they would be almost hopelessly behind at three games to one.

In those days, a ticket for a seat in the bleachers could be bought for 55 cents. It was a sweltering, 90-degree day, which is strange for October in the Northeast. The mayor of New York, Fiorello La Guardia, threw out the first ball. There was a banner in the stands at Ebbets Field that read: WE'VE WAITED 21 YEARS. DON'T FAIL US NOW.

THE DODGERS FELL BEHIND 3–0 early in the game and didn't get anything going until there were two out in the bottom of the fourth inning, when catcher Mickey Owen walked. Owen was a Missouri farm boy playing his first year with the Dodgers after being traded from the St. Louis Cardinals. He was born with the name Arnold, but took the name Mickey because he idolized Hall of Fame catcher Mickey Cochrane.

Second baseman Pete Coscarart followed Owen with another base on balls. Men on first and second, two outs. The Dodgers pitcher Larry French was due up next. Leo Durocher, who managed the team, decided that he needed to get some offense going, so he sent up Jim Wasdell to pinch-hit. Wasdell took an outside fastball and went the other way with it, slamming a drive into the left-field corner. It was fair by about a foot. Owen and Coscarart scored. Yankees 3, Dodgers 2.

In the next inning, the Dodgers got two more runs. Dixie Walker doubled to left. Pete Reiser was up next. Reiser, who was just 22, had come off a phenomenal season. He hit .343, making him the youngest batting champion in National League history. He also led the league in doubles (39), triples (17), and runs scored (117).

Reiser cranked up and unloaded a home run that cleared the right-field scoreboard and landed in Brooklyn's Bedford Avenue. It was the first Dodgers home run in the World Series since Hy Myers slammed one 25 years earlier. Dodgers 4, Yankees 3.

In the fifth inning, Durocher brought in his relief ace—Hugh Casey—to hold the Yankees. Casey, 14–11 for the season, was known for his good control and natural sinkerball. He didn't have much of a fastball and used it mainly to brush batters away from the plate.

Casey gave the Dodgers three brilliant innings. The Yankees could only manage a scratch single in the sixth and seventh innings. Casey sent them down in order in the eighth. Catcher Mickey Owen, who had the best view of the action, said Casey's curves "broke with a fork like the jagged end of summer lightning." Casey held the Yanks, and the score stayed 4–3.

That brings us to the top of the ninth inning—an inning many Dodgers fans *still* remember. It started out innocently enough. The Yankees first baseman Johnny Sturm ran the count full, then grounded out to second base. One out. Next, third baseman Red Rolfe tapped the ball back to the mound, and Hugh Casey threw him out. Two outs.

The Yankees were down to their last out. Tommy Henrich stepped up to the plate. His teammates called him Old Reliable because he came through so frequently in clutch situations—like this one.

Casey looked in for the sign from Owen, kicked up his left leg, and fired. The pitch missed, and umpire Larry Goetz called it a ball. Casey got the next one over, and Henrich didn't swing, so the count was 1–1. Henrich, a left-handed hitter, tightened his grip on the bat. There were no base runners, so Casey could focus all his attention on the batter. He split the plate again, and again Henrich didn't pull the trigger. Strike two.

The Yankees were now down to their last *strike.* Henrich didn't want to strike out, and he sure didn't want to make the final out of the game without taking a swing at the ball. With two strikes, he could no longer be choosy. He had to protect the plate. For the Dodgers, the game looked like it was in the bag.

Henrich fouled off the next pitch, then Casey wasted one off the outside corner. The next pitch was also off the plate for ball three. Full count.

Reporters in the press box noted that it was 4:35 in the afternoon. No more fooling around. Owen crouched down and gave Casey the sign—curveball, low, and on the inside corner. Casey nodded and went into his windup, twisting his wrist as he released the ball to make it spin and curve.

Henrich started to swing and then stopped, but it was too late. He was fooled and missed the ball badly. Umpire Goetz raised his hand to signal strike three. The game was over! Dodgers leaped out of the dugout to congratulate Casey, and some of the Yankees made their way to the showers. Security police leaped over the barricades to prevent any fans from rushing on the field.

BUT THE GAME *WASN'T* OVER. *Freeze this moment.*

Instead of shifting his feet to the right to catch the third strike on the inside corner, Mickey Owen reached over with his catcher's mitt, and the ball glanced off it.

According to the rules of baseball, if a catcher doesn't hold on to the third strike, he has to either tag the batter with the ball or throw him out at first base. Owen had set a National League record for consecutive errorless chances by a catcher earlier in the season and had only made three errors all year.

A lot of good that did him *now!* Frantically, Owen swerved around to find the ball. It rolled behind him, to the right of home plate. Henrich, disgusted at his strikeout, turned toward the Yankees dugout, where his teammates were yelling for him to run to first base. He sprinted madly out of the batter's box.

Ebbets Field in Brooklyn had dirt behind the plate, not grass, so the ball rolled all the way to the grandstand near the Dodgers dugout. That's where Owen finally retrieved it. Unfortunately, by the time he got his hand on the ball, Henrich was crossing first.

Years later, Leo Durocher said one of the biggest mistakes he ever made was not calling time and going out to the mound to calm down Hugh Casey and Mickey Owen. Like everyone else, the Dodgers manager was so shell-shocked by what had just happened that he couldn't think straight.

THE DODGERS WEREN'T DEAD YET. They still held a one-run lead with two outs in the ninth. Joe DiMaggio stepped up to the plate. If Casey could get him out, everybody would quickly forget about Mickey Owen's passed ball.

Casey reared back and fired a fastball, and DiMaggio ripped a single to left. The ball was hit so hard that Henrich could only advance to second. Charlie "King Kong" Keller was up next for the Yankees. He was a power hitter who was known to swing at a lot of bad balls. That's what Casey fed him, and Keller whiffed at two curveballs off the outside corner.

Once again the Dodgers were one strike away from winning the game. In the Brooklyn dugout, Leo Durocher whistled to get Casey's attention, then drew his hand across his chest. That was the sign to brush the batter back.

Instead, Casey threw one right down the middle. Durocher called it "the kind of pitch Keller saw about once a year." The Yankees slugger yanked the ball to the top of the left-field screen, just missing a home run. Henrich scored easily from second to tie the game up. DiMaggio scored all the way from first base, sliding neatly under Owen's tag. Yankees 5, Dodgers 4.

By then, Hugh Casey was furious and had lost all control. He walked Bill Dickey. Next, Joe Gordon doubled over Wasdell's head in left field, scoring Keller and Dickey. Yankees 7, Dodgers 4.

After the game *should* have been over, the Yankees had scored four runs! The Dodgers were stunned, and they finally got the third out and walked off the field.

In their half of the ninth inning, Yankees relief pitcher "Grandma" Murphy had no trouble disposing of Pee Wee Reese, Dixie Walker, and Pete Reiser to end the game for good.

Never in baseball history had a team come so close to winning and then blown it. Instead of the Series being tied up at two games each, the Yankees were ahead three games to one.

The next day the demoralized Dodgers could only manage four hits and one run off Tiny Bonham. They played like they just wanted to get the World Series over with. The Yankees had won their fifth championship in six years.

Once again, Brooklyn fans would go home mumbling, "Wait till next year." Actually, they would wait another 14 years, until the 1955 Dodgers finally won Brooklyn's first—and last—World Series.

What Happened Afterward

"IT WAS ALL MY FAULT," Mickey Owen said after the game. "It wasn't a strike. It was a great breaking curve— low, inside, and right at Henrich's shoe tops. I should have had it. But I guess the ball hit the side of my glove. It got away from me, and by the time I got hold of it near the corner of the dugout, I couldn't have thrown anybody out at first.

"I don't mind being the goat. I'm just sorry for what I cost the other guys."

Actually, Owen shouldn't have been so hard on himself. The "other guys," the rest of the Dodgers, hit a pathetic .182 in the World Series. Brooklyn's top hitter, Ducky Medwick, hit just .235.

Hugh Casey, who threw the fateful pitch, told reporters: "I guess I've lost 'em [ballgames] just about every way now. I never lost one by striking out a guy.

"With the count three and two on Henrich I figured I'd throw him a curve and put everything I had on the pitch. The ball really had a great break on it."

Years later, Casey admitted that the pitch he'd thrown Henrich wasn't a curveball, it was an illegal *spitball.* If that was true, and if he never told Owen he was throwing a spitter, Mickey could hardly be blamed for missing it. A spitball breaks down much more sharply than a curveball.

Tommy Henrich, the Yankees hitter, said: "It was a bad pitch, that three and two pitch. It came up nice and looked good, and I went for it. But when I started to swing I saw it going to break badly away from me and down. But I was going through with my swing. I couldn't stop it.

"That was a tough break for poor Mickey to get. I bet he feels like a nickel's worth of dog meat."

Joe DiMaggio summed the game up nicely. "Well," he said, "they say everything happens in Brooklyn."

AFTER THE SEASON, Mickey Owen received more than five thousand letters of encouragement from people all over the country. "The missed third strike, instead of ruining my career, will make me a better catcher not only during this new season of 1942, but until the day I hang up my mask and glove forever," he wrote in an article that appeared in *Collier's* magazine that year.

After a productive career, Mickey Owen retired from baseball following the 1954 season. In 1960, he founded the Mickey Owen Baseball School for Boys in Missouri. He was the County Sheriff of Greene County, Missouri, from 1964 until 1980. Friends wanted him to run for Congress but he said he'd traveled enough in his baseball days.

Lifetime Statistics

MICKEY OWEN: Years 13, games 1,209, batting average .255, fielding average .981, home runs 14, stolen bases 36.

Did You Know . . .

◆ The same season, Mickey Owen handled 476 chances without an error.

◆ On August 4 of that season, Owen caught three foul pop-ups in a single inning. That's a record that, obviously, will never be broken.

◆ On August 3, 1937, Owen made an unassisted double play, which is very rare for a catcher.

◆ The Dodgers got their name because there were so many streetcars in Brooklyn that the people came to be called "trolley dodgers." In 1958, the Dodgers moved to Los Angeles, where there are no trolleys.

◆ When the Dodgers left Brooklyn, heartbroken fans went to Ebbets Field to collect spades of dirt, clumps of grass, bleacher seats, and other reminders of their beloved team. The stadium was eventually torn down, and apartment buildings stand on that spot today.

◆ Before 1958, New York City had three major league baseball teams—the Dodgers, the Giants, and the Yankees. After the Dodgers and Giants moved to California, New York politicians attempted to form a third major league so that New York would have another team. The Continental League never played a game, but one of the proposed teams became the New York Mets. The Mets colors—blue and orange—were a combination of team colors from the old New York Giants and Brooklyn Dodgers.

◆ Mickey Owen was not the only ballplayer named in honor of Mickey Cochrane. A coal miner named Mutt Mantle named his son Mickey after Cochrane, too, and Mickey Mantle joined Mickey Cochrane in the Baseball Hall of Fame.

Also in 1941 . . .

◆ Joe DiMaggio got at least one hit in 56 consecutive games.

◆ Ted Williams hit .406, becoming the last batter to average .400 in a season.

◆ Arky Vaughan hit two homers in the All-Star Game.

◆ Lou Gehrig passed away after two years of suffering with a rare spinal disease that came to be called Lou Gehrig's Disease.

CHAPTER
4

The Buckner Boot

THE DATE: Thursday, October 25, 1986.
THE PLACE: Shea Stadium, New York City.
THE SITUATION: The New York Mets
versus the Boston Red Sox. Game 6 of
the World Series. Bottom of the tenth,
tie score, two outs, full count.

Bill Buckner (George Brace)

ild pitch, error
n Sox in 10th

scarelli
ter

Mets Force the Final Game With Dramatic Rall

K

The Mets were delirious after Buckner's error allowed them to come from behind to win. They had been one strike away from losing the World Series. (AP/Wide World Photos)

Game 7

*T*HE AMAZING STORY of Bill Buckner's big boot in 1986 actually begins a long time ago—on January 5, 1920. That was the day Boston Red Sox owner Harry Frazee sold a 24-year-old pitcher/slugger named Babe Ruth to the New York Yankees for $100,000. It was undoubtedly the stupidest deal in all of baseball history. From that day on, it is said, the Babe Ruth Curse would forever haunt Boston and prevent the Red Sox from winning the World Series.

It sounds crazy, but look at the facts: Before Ruth was sold, Boston was a powerhouse, winning five of the first 15 World Series. The Bambino personally led the team to the title in 1916 and 1918. Since Ruth left Boston, however, the Red Sox have not won a *single* World Series.

Before Ruth arrived on the Yankees, no New York team had won a World Series. Afterward, the Yankees became the most dominating dynasty in the history of sports, and New York teams (Yankees, Dodgers, Giants, Mets) have won the World Series 29 times.

It's not that Boston fielded bad baseball teams all those years. The Red Sox have almost always been in the pennant race, but they always seemed to collapse or choke when the chips were down. Twice they lost one-game playoffs to decide the American League pennant (1948 and 1978). Every time they made it to the

World Series (1946, 1967, and 1975), they lost it in the seventh game.

It's almost as if the ghost of the Sultan of Swat has been watching over Boston all these years, making sure the Sox never win it all.

The Red Sox were never closer to breaking the Babe Ruth Curse than in 1986, and this is where the Buckner Boot fits in.

Boston won the first two games of the World Series, and the New York Mets won the next two. Game 5 went to the Sox, putting Boston ahead three games to two. One more victory and the Red Sox would be World Champions for the first time since 1918.

Sixty-eight years. That's a long time to wait. People had been born, lived their lives, and died of natural causes since the Red Sox had won. The last time the Sox were World Champions, Woodrow Wilson was President of the United States.

Game 6, to be known forever as "the Buckner Game," was one for the ages. *The New York Times* called it "one of the classics in the 83-year history of the World Series." *Sports Illustrated* reviewed the game as though it was a theatrical performance: "an improbable melodrama, wild and ragged, desperate and fierce, heart-breaking and heart-lifting." The magazine called it "one of the most thrilling in Series history."

Writers usually keep their own experiences out of stories like this, but I hope you'll forgive me for breaking that rule here. I've been a Mets fan since I was ten, and Game 6 was the most exciting experience I've ever had watching a sporting event. I watched the game on TV in Princeton, New Jersey, during a visit to my sister and brother-in-law. I'll try not to get *too* carried away describing it.

ONE MORE WIN IN THE SERIES and the Sox would be World Champs. Fireballer Roger Clemens (24–4) started the game for Boston; Bob Ojeda (18–5) for the Mets. Right off the bat, something took place that hinted that this game was going to be memorable. In the top of the first inning, Ojeda was about to pitch to Bill Buckner when people in the stands suddenly began pointing up in the air. The camera panned around until it picked up a canary yellow parachute floating down into the stadium. The parachutist, with a LET'S GO METS banner trailing behind him, landed near the pitcher's mound. He was led away by police through the Mets dugout.

Ojeda, Buckner, and everybody else shook their heads in wonder. Later, the sky would fall in on Bill Buckner in another way.

Clemens was awesome, pitching a no-hitter through four innings. His fastball was clocked at 95 miles per hour or *faster* on 27 pitches. Ojeda, more of a finesse pitcher, looked like he was throwing in slow motion next to the Rocket Man.

It was a seesaw battle. The Red Sox scored a run in the first and another in the second. The Mets struck back with two in the fifth to tie it. The Sox then scored another run in the seventh. The Mets got it back in the eighth.

Clemens had thrown a hundred pitches by the sixth inning, which is about the limit for most pitchers in one day. A blister developed on the middle finger of his pitching hand, and it was bleeding. At the end of the seventh inning, Clemens's pitch count had reached 137, and Red Sox manager John McNamara decided to take him out. Mets manager Davey Johnson lifted Ojeda after six innings. A battle of the bullpens would decide the game.

In Princeton, my wife, Nina, absentmindedly picked a grapefruit out of a bowl just as Lee Mazzilli lined a single to right for the Mets in the eighth. When Maz scored the tying run, we naturally dubbed it "the lucky grapefruit" and determined that Nina would hold it for the rest of the game.

Not that we're superstitious, mind you. But it certainly couldn't *hurt* to hold a grapefruit while watching a ball game, could it?

At the end of nine innings, the game was still tied up at 3–3. Boston, remember, held a 3–2 lead in games, so one run could win the World Series for them. Every pitch was filled with tension.

Dave Henderson led off the top of the tenth inning for Boston. A week earlier, the Red Sox had been down to their last strike in the American League Championship Series when Henderson slugged a two-run home run. The Sox went on to win that game, and the following two as well to win the pennant.

Mets pitcher Rick Aguilera must have been thinking about that as he went into his windup, but it didn't stop Hendu. He clubbed an 0–1 fastball off the auxiliary scoreboard in left for a home run. Boston 4, New York 3. I was beginning to think the lucky grapefruit wasn't so lucky after all. The scoreboard clock flashed twelve midnight as Henderson crossed the plate.

Aguilera struck out the next two batters, but Wade Boggs doubled and Marty Barrett singled to add an insurance run. Boston 5, New York 3. Now I was *sure* the lucky grapefruit wasn't lucky. It looked like the end of the line for the Mets. A few discouraged Mets fans headed for their cars to beat the traffic out of Shea Stadium.

Red Sox fans couldn't hide their joy. In homes, restaurants, and bars all over Boston, they were going nuts. The Red Sox were *actually* going to win the World Series.

The Babe Ruth Curse was finally dead. Car horns were heard honking on the Massachusetts Turnpike.

Television broadcaster Bob Costas and his NBC crew began setting up for the historic post-game interviews in the Red Sox clubhouse. Twenty cases of champagne were wheeled in, along with the World Series trophy. The scoreboard operator at Shea Stadium hit the wrong button and the words CONGRATULATIONS BOSTON RED SOX appeared momentarily on the scoreboard.

NEW YORK CAME UP for its last licks in the bottom of the tenth. Calvin Schiraldi, who had been with the Mets a season earlier, was on the mound for Boston.

The first batter, Wally Backman, flied out to left field. Keith Hernandez, the Mets' best clutch hitter, flied out to deep center. Hernandez threw down his batting helmet in disgust and stormed into the Mets clubhouse. He couldn't bear to watch the sad ending. In the Boston clubhouse, the players' cubicles were draped with plastic to protect them from spraying champagne in the celebration that was surely about to take place.

The Mets were two runs behind and down to their last out. It would take a miracle at this point. The Red Sox players were standing in the dugout, ready to run out on the field to celebrate. Oil Can Boyd, a Boston pitcher, was doing a little slamdance. Bob Costas was informed that he was to announce that the Most Valuable Player in the World Series was Boston pitcher Bruce Hurst.

I ripped the unlucky grapefruit out of Nina's hands and sank into my gloom on the couch. If she hadn't been holding the stupid grapefruit, I thought logically, the Mets would probably be *winning*.

Mets catcher Gary Carter stepped up to the plate. He knew one thing—he didn't want to make the last out in the World Series. Carter had caught Schiraldi when he was with the Mets and knew his strengths and weaknesses. When Schiraldi threw the first pitch under Carter's chin, the veteran catcher stepped out of the batter's box for a moment to glare at the young pitcher. They played cat and mouse for two pitches, and with a 2–1 count Carter dumped a little single into left field.

The Mets were still alive. It was up to pitcher Rick Aguilera to make the last out.

New York manager Davey Johnson called for Kevin Mitchell to pinch-hit. The only problem was that Mitchell was already in the clubhouse, completely naked, making plane reservations for his trip home after the game. Mitchell threw his uniform back on and hustled out to the the batter's box.

The first pitch was a fastball up and in. Mitchell let

it go by. The next one was a slider low and away. The muscular outfielder found it more to his liking and poked a single to left. Carter stopped at second.

Schiraldi was starting to look a little nervous, and Red Sox pitching coach Bill Fischer trotted out to the mound to settle him down. It seemed to work. Schiraldi got two quick strikes on third baseman Ray Knight. The Mets were down to their last strike. Their season could be over on the next pitch.

Ahead on the count, Schiraldi threw what *should* have been a teaser off the corner of the plate. But Knight reached over and blooped a broken-bat single to center. Carter came around from second to score, making it 5–4. Kevin Mitchell alertly advanced to third. From the on-deck circle, Mookie Wilson watched.

Three singles in a row. The tying run was 90 feet away. Long-time Boston fans began to experience a familiar sinking feeling in the pit of their stomachs. The Red Sox had blown it so many times before. Could they possibly lose this ball game?

Out went Schiraldi. In came Bob Stanley. He was called the Steamer after the Stanley Steamer, a steam-powered automobile that was popular in Babe Ruth's day.

Of course, cars that ran on hot air never made it.

As Stanley was warming up, Mets third base coach

Bud Harrelson whispered to Kevin Mitchell to be on the alert for a wild pitch. That wasn't likely, however—Stanley had tossed just one in 94 innings during the regular season.

What followed was one of the most gripping at-bats in baseball history—a ten-pitch war, with hitter and pitcher like two boxers slugging it out at the bell. Stanley versus Wilson for baseball's heavyweight title. One of them would hit the canvas. Wilson was like the boxer with his back to the ropes, fending off blows that would knock out the Mets. The crowd was screaming on each delivery.

This was the pitch sequence . . .

1. The first delivery was high and outside, but Mookie Wilson was a free swinger and took a cut at it. 0–1.

2. Ball one. 1–1.

3. Ball two. Outside. 2–1.

4. Foul ball, strike two. 2–2 count. Again, the Mets were down to their last strike. Several of the Red Sox were poised with one foot in the dugout and the other up on the field ready to charge and begin the celebration. Security police prepared to take control of the field and prevent a riot.

5. Mookie fouled off a breaking ball. 2–2. The New York crowd was screaming for him to stay alive.

6. Mookie fouled off *another* breaking ball. 2–2. Tension was mounting with each pitch.

7. Stanley decided to throw an inside fastball that would tail away from the batter, toward the plate. Just one problem—it didn't tail. The ball stayed inside, heading for Mookie's rib cage. Wilson jackknifed out of the way. (He's still hovering in midair, in my mind.) The ball glanced off the mitt of catcher Rich Gedman and bounded away.

"Go! Go! Go!" Harrelson yelled. Kevin Mitchell scored from third standing up. Incredibly, the Mets had tied the game. Ray Knight moved up to second on the wild pitch. In living rooms and dens across America and around the world, people couldn't believe what they were seeing. I gripped the lucky grapefruit as if it was a life preserver.

The overanxious Red Sox sat back down in their dugout with a collective thud. In the Boston clubhouse, Bob Costas and the NBC crew packed up their equipment and whisked out of there like the place was under attack. Red Sox fans were saying to themselves, "It was only a matter of time." Somewhere, the ghost of Babe Ruth was chuckling.

8. The count was full. Mookie Wilson relaxed a little bit at the plate. Instead of being in position to make the

last out, he was in position to *win the game.* Now it was
Stanley who was under pressure. Wilson's bat seemed
to have only foul balls in it, so he went and got a new
piece of lumber. No matter; he fouled off another pitch,
back behind the plate. 3–2.

9. Foul down the third-base line. 3–2.

10. Stanley threw a fastball on the inside corner. Wilson
swung and topped a crazily bouncing grounder up the
first-base line. Mets first base coach Bill Robinson said
to himself, "Go foul, ball."

FREEZE THIS MOMENT. Bill Buckner was playing
first. After 18 years in the big leagues, his legs were shot.
High-topped baseball shoes covered bone spurs and se-
verely damaged ligaments in both his ankles, and it was
painful just to *watch* him run.

Before the World Series, a "holy woman" had sent
Buckner an elixir she believed would heal him. Figuring
he'd tried everything else, Buckner drank half of the
stuff. Maybe he should have downed the whole thing.

Buckner was playing close to the first-base line and
deep, nearly thirty feet behind the bag. The ball bounced
inches from the base. He only had to move a step or two
to the left to get his body in front of it. Bob Stanley raced
off the mound to cover first in case Buckner couldn't

make the play unassisted. Mookie Wilson was fast. It was going to be close.

Playing so deep, Buckner knew that he didn't have time to get down on his knees to block the ball, the way first basemen are taught, and still make a strong throw to Stanley at first base. He didn't charge the ball. Instead, he stooped down for it with his legs apart.

Maybe Buckner took his eye off the ball for a split second. Maybe he was rushed and not as careful as he should have been. Maybe the pressure got to him. In any case, the ball bounced three times and then slipped under his glove and between his legs like a boat under a drawbridge. He never touched it. My eyes bugged out of my head as I held the lucky grapefruit and yelled my head off.

Heartbroken, Buckner hobbled off the field. (Sports Illustrated)

Ray Knight raced home with the winning run. The Mets had evened the Series at three games apiece. As the Mets and their fans whooped and hollered, the camera lingered on Wade Boggs in the Boston dugout. He was weeping as if—as if his team had the World Championship in the palm of its hand and let it slip away.

"I can't remember the last time I missed a ground ball," Bill Buckner told reporters after the game. "I'll remember that one."

TWO DAYS LATER, the Mets and the Red Sox went at it again in the seventh and deciding game. Again the Mets came from behind, with three runs in the sixth inning, to win it all. They became only the second team in World Series history to lose the first two games at home and come back to win. (The Kansas City Royals did it just the year before.)

The Mets owed it all, of course, to my lucky grapefruit.

What Happened Afterward

IT'S TOO SOON TO TELL, but the Buckner Boot may outlive Merkle, Snodgrass, Owen, and all the others in this book as the most dramatic muff in baseball history. "Until Saturday, Mickey Owen had been rated the World Series' top goat," wrote *Sports Illustrated* in its wrapup of the Series. "Alas, now there is a new kid on the block."

Bill Buckner jokes were on the street almost immediately, the best of which were . . .

Q. What do Bill Buckner and Michael Jackson have in common?
A. They both wear a glove on one hand for no apparent reason.

Q. Did you hear that Bill Buckner slipped and fell onto the Boston subway tracks?
A. Yeah, but he's okay—the train went between his legs.

Every sportscaster provided an analysis of the fateful grounder, but only two viewpoints mattered—Mookie Wilson's and Bill Buckner's.

"Once the ball got past the bag, I thought I had a chance to beat the throw," Wilson said.

"I knew it was going to be a close play at first because the guy runs so well," explained Buckner. "The ball went skip, skip, skip and didn't come up. It just missed my glove. I've got to live with it."

Boston manager John McNamara had to live with it too. He took a lot of criticism for not putting in a defensive replacement for Buckner in the late innings of the game. In three of the previous five games, he had taken out Buckner and put in Dave Stapleton to protect the Boston lead. Buckner had been hit by a pitch in the Red Sox half of the tenth, and that would have been the perfect time to replace him with a pinch runner.

McNamara never admitted he'd made a mistake. Some said Buckner talked him out of making a change. Others speculated that McNamara left Buckner on the field so he would be in the victory photos. When reporters brought up the Babe Ruth Curse, McNamara would say glumly, "I don't know nothin' about history."

BILL BUCKNER WAS TRADED to the California Angels the next season. He played for four more years and retired, at the age of 40 in 1990. Incredibly, in his last season he played again for the Red Sox.

As for the Boston Red Sox, it's now 74 years without a World Series victory, and counting. The Babe Ruth Curse lives!

And as for the lucky grapefruit, it had become lopsided and rotten a week after the World Series was over. I thought about bronzing it or something but decided that would be silly. Instead, Nina and I held it solemnly, and ceremoniously dumped it in a garbage can. It had served its purpose.

Lifetime Statistics

BILL BUCKNER: Years 22, games 2,517, batting average .289, fielding average .991, home runs 174, hits 2,715, RBIs 1,208, doubles 498, stolen bases 183.

Did You Know . . .

♦ Playing for the Cubs, Bill Buckner won the National League batting championship in 1980, hitting .324.

♦ Buckner hit best in even-numbered years: 1972 (.319), 1974 (.314), 1976 (.301), 1978 (.323), 1980 (.324). In every odd-numbered year within that span, he was below .300.

♦ Buckner led the National League in doubles in 1981 and 1983. In 1982, he led the league in at-bats with 657.

♦ The man who parachuted into Shea Stadium at the start of this game was an actor named Michael Sergio. After he landed, he slapped hands with Mets pitcher Ron Darling near the Mets dugout. Then he was handcuffed and arrested. He refused to tell the Federal Aviation Administration who flew the plane, and he pleaded guilty to criminal trespassing and reckless endangerment.

♦ This was the Mets' second World Championship in their 25-year history. Within a few years of winning this

Series, the stars of the team—Hernandez, Carter, Mitch-ell, Knight, Wilson—scattered to other teams by trades or free agency.

◆ The Most Valuable Player of this World Series—Ray Knight—is married to professional golfer Nancy Lopez.

◆ Red Sox third baseman Wade Boggs hit .290 in this World Series, but won the American League batting title in 1983 (.361), 1985 (.368), 1986 (.357), 1987 (.363), and 1988 (.366). He has never hit under .300 in his ten-year career.

Also in 1986 . . .

◆ Pete Rose never officially retired, but played his last game, leading all major leaguers in hits, games, and at-bats.

◆ Don Sutton won his three hundredth game.

◆ Greg Gagne of the Minnesota Twins hit two inside-the-park home runs in one game.

◆ Don Baylor set the American League record by get-ting hit with pitches 35 times throughout the season.

◆ Pitchers Phil Niekro (of the Cleveland Indians) and Don Sutton (of the California Angels) were the two start-ing pitchers in a game—the first duel between three-hundred game winners since 1892.

◆ The split-finger fastball was popularized by pitching coach Roger Craig.

Other Legendary
Bloops and Blunders

CHAPTER
5

Heinie Zimmerman's
Dash to the Plate

THE DATE: Monday, October 15, 1917.
THE PLACE: The Polo Grounds,
New York City.
THE SITUATION: Game 6 of the World
Series between the New York Giants and
the Chicago White Sox. Fourth inning.
Men on first and third. Nobody out.

He called himself "The Great Zim." (NBL)

TE SOX TAKE
RLD TITLE IN
ORRID FINISH

Chicago American League Team
Wins the Deciding Series
Game by 4 to 2.

ZIM'S BLUNDERS ARE FATAL

Heinie's Misplays in Fourth Inning Send New York Crash-
ing on Way to Defeat.

BENTON PITCHES BRAVELY

*Heinie snared this one, but in the 1917 World Series
his pathetic footrace against Eddie Collins
had the fans howling with laughter. (NBL)*

*I*N THE 1917 WORLD SERIES, the goat's horns belonged to Henry "Heinie" Zimmerman, third baseman for the New York Giants. Zimmerman, for a while at least, was one of the best players in the game. He won the National League Triple Crown (batting title, RBI leader, home run leader) in 1912 and led the league in RBIs for three seasons.

Heinie knew he was good, and called himself the Great Zim. But *The New York Times* called him a "dunce" and said he had made "one of the stupidest plays that had ever been seen in a World Series."

Of course, that was 66 years ago. There have been plenty of stupid plays since then that could easily challenge Heinie Zimmerman for the top spot.

Heinie started his bad-luck streak in Game 5, when he made two errors. After one of them, the White Sox punched out four straight singles and turned a 5–5 tie into an 8–5 defeat for the Giants. This enabled the White Sox to take a 3–2 lead in the Series.

A group of White Sox fans came to the stadium with a gift for Zimmerman that day—a box of raspberries, which they hurled at him every time he came to bat or took the field.

It was in Game 6 that Zimmerman made the play that baseball fans would remember long after he had left the game. It came to be called Zimmerman's Chase.

UP UNTIL THE FOURTH INNING, Game 6 was a
scoreless pitcher's battle between Rube Benton of the
Giants and Urban Faber of the White Sox. Eddie Collins
(.409 for the Series) led off in the fourth for the White
Sox. He hit a routine grounder toward third base. Zimmerman scooped it up and promptly threw the ball in
the dirt far in front of first base. It skittered past first
baseman Walter Holke and into right field. Collins
pulled into second. Another error for Heinie.

Next up was the legendary Shoeless Joe Jackson,
who lofted an easy fly ball to right. The right fielder,
Dave Robertson, moved in a few steps, camped under
the ball . . . and dropped it. Collins advanced to third,
and Jackson was safe at first.

That's two Giant errors in a row. If Rube Benton was
steamed at his teammates, he tried not to show it. Happy
Felsch was up for the White Sox. Benton threw him a
curveball, and Felsch fouled it into the right-field stands.
Benton tried another curve, and this time Felsch slapped
a high bounding ball back to the pitcher.

FREEZE THIS MOMENT. Runners on first and third,
nobody out, grounder to the pitcher. Nine times out of
ten, a team will go for the easy double play in a situation
like this. That lets the runner on third score, but chokes

off a big rally. After all, it was only the fourth inning, so there was plenty of time to catch up.

Benton picked up the grounder cleanly. He glanced over to third for a moment and saw that Eddie Collins was almost halfway between third and home. At that moment, Benton decided to ignore the double play and get Collins instead.

Benton ran toward the third-base line to chase Collins back to the bag. Collins, caught by surprise and knowing he was a dead duck, waved frantically for his teammates Jackson and Felsch to advance as far as they could while he was in the rundown. The Giants closed in on Collins.

Any Little Leaguer knows that in a rundown play you're supposed to maneuver the runner back to the base where he started and tag him out there. Benton, properly, chased Collins toward third and whipped the ball over to Zimmerman. Collins, naturally, changed directions and moved away from third.

Zimmerman tossed the ball to Giants catcher Bill Rariden, who chased Collins toward third again and tossed the ball back to Zimmerman.

Most base runners would have been nailed by this time. But Eddie Collins, who stole 743 bases in his career and would become a Hall of Famer, was no average base runner. As soon as Rariden tossed the ball to Zimmerman, Collins headed in the other direction and sprinted toward the plate. Zimmerman was one step behind him.

"Throw the ball!" screamed every player on the Giants bench and a good number of fans. Rariden, the catcher, waited for the return throw from Zimmerman, but it never came.

Instead, Zimmerman decided to have a footrace to the plate with Collins. Both men took off, Heinie holding the ball in front of him in his outstretched hand, inches from Collins's back.

If the two men had been equally swift runners, it might have been a close race. But Collins was much faster than Zimmerman, and the race was a mismatch.

"At the halfway mark Collins was gathering speed and gaining in every jump," reported *The New York Times*. "Heinie's feet were behaving as if they were having a hard time keeping out of each other's way."

Collins scooted across the plate to score, with Zimmerman lumbering behind. Heinie had built up such a head of steam that he ran twenty feet past home plate before he was able to turn around. By that time, Joe Jackson had advanced to third base and Happy Felsch to second.

The newspapers of the day reported that the crowd shook with laughter, and that the White Sox were so joyous that "they hopped around like jumping jacks."

"It looked for a moment as if the Giants were going to form a posse and haul Zim to the tar barrel," wrote the *Times*.

The next man up, Chick Gandil, swung at the first pitch and ripped a single down the right-field line to score Jackson and Felsch.

The Giants never caught up. Final score: Chicago 4, New York 2. The White Sox were the World Champions. Rube Benton, who had not given up a single earned run in 14 innings of the World Series, was the losing pitcher.

What Happened Afterward

HEINIE ZIMMERMAN was to spend the rest of his life trying to convince the world that he wasn't to blame for the muffed play. He may have been right. When there's a rundown between third base and home, the pitcher and first baseman are supposed to be behind the plate to help cover it in case the catcher is out of position. But when Zimmerman began his famous chase, he looked at home plate and saw just one man there— umpire Bill Klem. Pitcher Rube Benton and first baseman Walter Holke were standing at their positions watching the action as if they were spectators.

"Who should I have thrown the ball to," Zimmerman would ask anyone who would listen, "Klem?"

It was New York Giants manager John McGraw's

fourth straight World Series loss, and he left the club-house fifteen minutes after the game was over. McGraw never blamed Fred Merkle for losing the 1908 pennant or Fred Snodgrass for losing the 1912 World Series, and he didn't blame Zimmerman either. He blamed Walter Holke for not covering home plate on the play.

There was plenty of blame to go around. If Dave Robertson hadn't dropped the easy fly ball, Collins would never have been on third base to begin with. And if Rube Benton had taken the easy double play, the Giants would have given up just one run and had two outs with the bases clear. If you look at the box score, you'll see that Zimmerman was not given an error for the play.

Nevertheless, the sportswriters made Heinie out to be the biggest laughingstock in baseball since the two Freds—Merkle and Snodgrass. It didn't help that Zimmerman was also a bust with a bat, hitting .120 for the Series in the cleanup position.

INTERESTINGLY, ten men on these two teams were banned from baseball for life two years later. After the 1919 World Series, it was discovered that eight White Sox players (Joe Jackson, Chick Gandil, Happy Felsch, Eddie Cicotte, Buck Weaver, Fred McMullin, Swede Risberg, and Lefty Williams) had intentionally lost the

Series for gamblers. This was the Black Sox Scandal, baseball's most notorious black mark.

On the New York Giants, center fielder Benny Kauff was banned for life when it was discovered he had been involved in a stolen car ring.

And Heinie Zimmerman—the Great Zim—was banished from baseball forever when it was discovered that he and teammate Hal Chase had accepted money from gamblers to throw ball games. He became a steamfitter and passed away in 1969, in New York City.

Lifetime Statistics

HEINIE ZIMMERMAN: Years 13, games 1,456, batting average .295, fielding average .933, home runs 58, stolen bases 175.

Did You Know . . .

♦ Besides winning the Triple Crown in 1912, Zimmerman also led the National League in hits (207), doubles (41), total bases (318), and slugging percentage (.571).

♦ Zimmerman hit 20 or more doubles eight times and ten or more triples six times.

♦ Zimmerman stole home 13 times in his career, placing him twentieth on the all-time list.

♦ Joe Jackson, who was on second base during Zimmerman's chase, was immortalized recently in two movies—*Field of Dreams* and *Eight Men Out.* The story about his not wearing shoes is false. Shoeless Joe *did* wear shoes. But it *is* true that he didn't know how to read or write.

♦ The last surviving Black Soxer was Swede Risberg, who passed away in 1975.

Also in 1917 . . .

♦ Fred Toney of Cincinnati and Hippo Vaughn of the Chicago Cubs both pitched no-hitters through nine innings in a game against one another. Vaughn lost it in the tenth.

♦ Hank Gowdy of the Boston Braves became the first major leaguer to enlist in the service (see next chapter).

SENATORS WIN WORLI

ROWDS HE
VICTORY (

emonstration (
Johnson Was
Game When

APITAL I
IN HOUR (

Washington's
Since Signin
Attend Sena

OHNSON HEI

housands We
Idol After Gar
Continues F

CITY A BED

annon Roar,
and Sirens Scr
Street Crowc

RESIDENT URGED
TO DINE CHAMPI

TEAM
SAYS

Washing
Hardly

JOHNSC

"They C
Comme
to Y

Spec
WASHI
danced t
stalked a
the grand
The Sen
laughed a
a holiday
downcast
"I can'
that we a
Stanley I
had out
McGraw.
bully on
have eve
ning. B
realize t
there an
"We p
repaid u
through

CAPITAL WILD WITH

CHAPTER

6

Hank Gowdy
Steps in It

THE DATE: Friday, October 10, 1924.
THE PLACE: Griffith Stadium,
Washington, D.C.
THE SITUATION: Game 7 of the World
Series between the New York Giants and
the Washington Senators. Top of the
twelfth inning. Tie score.

Hank Gowdy, when he was a hero for the Braves. (NBL)

*Gowdy stupidly got his foot stuck on his own mask, and once again
the New York Giants botched the World Series. (NBL)*

SOMETIMES YOU'RE THE HERO, sometimes you're the goat. Hank Gowdy, a little-known catcher whose career spanned 1910–30, had the distinction of being a hero *and* a goat in the World Series.

Gowdy was the star of the 1914 Series for the Boston Braves when he hit an astonishing .545 in the four-game sweep over Connie Mack's Philadelphia Athletics. He was unstoppable, collecting a home run, a triple, three doubles, a single, and six walks in 11 official times at bat (walks don't count as at-bats). Nobody had ever hit better than .500 in a World Series before Gowdy.

Ten years later, in the 1924 World Series, Hank Gowdy made what was perhaps the most humiliating error in World Series history. Once *again*, a freak accident would cause the New York Giants to lose a championship.

IT HAPPENED IN THE FINAL INNING of the final game. The Giants pitcher Virgil Barnes had been making the Senators look like a bunch of Little Leaguers. Going into the eighth inning the Giants were ahead 3–1, thanks to two Washington errors in the sixth. Six more outs and the World Championship would belong to John McGraw and the Giants for the third time in four years.

The Senators got two men on base when Nemo Leibold (how's that for a name?) doubled and Muddy Ruel singled. Bucky Harris, Washington's 27-year-old boy-wonder player/manager, stepped up to the plate.

It should be mentioned here that before Harris took over the team, Washington was always known for being "first in war, first in peace, and last in the American League." In their 35-year history, the Senators had never come within shouting distance of winning the pennant. The previous year they finished a whopping 24 games behind.

Harris slapped a hard grounder to third. It looked like an easy play, but the ball hit a pebble and took a bad hop, skipping a foot over the head of Giants third baseman Fred Lindstrom. Two runs scored and the game was tied at 3–3.

In the ninth inning, Harris brought in the immortal Walter Johnson as a relief pitcher. Big Train, as he was called, had pitched his heart out to win 374 games in 18 seasons for the hapless Senators. Finally he was getting the chance to play in his first World Series. Johnson had already lost Game 1 and Game 5.

Johnson held the Giants through the ninth, tenth, and eleventh innings. The Giants pitcher Jack Bentley wasn't any easier on the Senators.

Then came the top of the twelfth, an inning baseball fans still talk about nearly seventy years later. Ralph Miller hit a short grounder to second that Frank Frisch picked up and threw to first. One out. Muddy Ruel, the Washington catcher, came to the plate. Ruel's single in the eighth had been his first hit of the Series. He didn't seem to be much of a threat with a .050 average.

BENTLEY WENT INTO HIS WINDUP, and Ruel took a mighty swing. *Freeze this moment.* Ruel must have just nicked the bottom of the ball, because it went straight up in the air, very high. Hank Gowdy ripped off his catcher's mask quickly and looked up to follow the path of the ball.

The ball drifted back about ten feet behind home plate. Gowdy drifted with it, tossing his mask aside at the same time. Every catcher is trained to toss the mask as far away as possible to avoid tripping over it. The pop foul was very high and Gowdy had to circle around below it to get the ball in his sights. It looked like an easy out.

Suddenly, the wind kicked up and blew the ball *back* toward the plate—and back where the catcher's mask lay on the ground. Gowdy moved forward under the ball. Just as it was starting to come down, his foot came down

on top of the mask. His toe became firmly lodged between the bars.

Like a wounded animal caught in a trap, Gowdy
tried to shake the mask off his foot. At the same time,
the ball was streaking toward him. He stumbled and
fell, losing sight of the ball. It dropped harmlessly on
the grass a few feet away.

A THOUSAND HEARTS skipped a beat. It couldn't be
happening to the New York Giants *again!* Catchers don't
get their feet caught in their own masks. It just didn't
happen. But it had.

As so often occurs after a botched foul pop, the batter
took advantage. Muddy Ruel, hardly believing his good
luck, banged a double down the left-field line. Washington had the run that would win the World Series in
scoring position.

Walter Johnson stepped up to the plate. What a fit-
ting ending it would be for the veteran pitcher, perhaps
playing in his last game, to win it with a base hit.

Johnson didn't get a hit. He slapped a grounder to
Travis Jackson at short. Distracted by Muddy Ruel danc-
ing off second base, Jackson fumbled the ball. Ruel held
at second. Instead of three outs, there was just one out
and men on first and second. The Washington crowd

could taste victory. On the mound, Jack Bentley must have been wondering what he had to do to get somebody out. He prepared to face Earl McNeely, the Senators center fielder.

McNeely chopped a routine grounder to Fred Lindstrom at third. The sun was streaming in through the back of the stands at that moment, right into Lindstrom's eyes. Incredibly, lightning struck twice. The ball took a bad hop off a pebble, just as it had in the eighth inning, and bounced over Lindstrom's head. Muddy Ruel came around from second to score easily.

The left fielder, Irish Meusel, didn't even make a throw. He just picked up the ball and put it in his pocket. The Washington Senators were the World Champions for the first (and, as it turned out, last) time ever. Walter Johnson got his World Series win, and President Calvin Coolidge and his wife were there to see it, enjoying their third game in the Series.

What Happened Afterward

HANK GOWDY got the blame for the World Series loss, even though Fred Lindstrom missed two grounders that brought in three of the Senators' four runs. Most likely, it was because Gowdy looked so ridiculous hopping around trying to catch a foul pop with his mask stuck on his foot.

"In years to come they will call Gowdy's failure the $50,000 muff," reported *The New York Times*.

"I've been in baseball thirty years and that's the first time I ever saw a catcher step into his own mask," said Christy Mathewson. "Everything bad seems to happen to Giant teams in the World Series."

First it was Merkle in 1908, then Snodgrass in 1912, and Zimmerman in 1917. And now Gowdy in 1924. There seemed to be a jinx working against the New York Giants. They always found a way to make the big mistake. In 32 years under John McGraw's command, the Giants reached the World Series nine times, but only won three of them.

This was to be McGraw's last pennant. After eight frustrating years without reaching first place again, he resigned in 1932. He died two years later.

Hank Gowdy retired from baseball the year after his big blunder, but then made a brief comeback in 1929.

Lifetime Statistics

HANK GOWDY: Years 17, games 1,050, batting average .270, fielding average .975, home runs 21.

Did You Know . . .

◆ Hank Gowdy was born (1889) and died (1966) in the same town—Columbus, Ohio.

◆ During World War I, Gowdy served in the Rainbow Division at Chateau-Thierry, St. Mihiel, and Argonne. These were some of the bloodiest battles of the war.

◆ Gowdy managed the Cincinnati Reds in 1946, his only stint as manager.

◆ Gowdy, as catcher, made an unassisted double play on May 1, 1920.

◆ Gowdy caught two no-hitters with Boston, one for George Davis in 1914 and another one two years later for Tom Hughes.

◆ Gowdy hit just 21 home runs in 17 years in the majors. He slammed four in 1924, his best year ever in that department.

◆ Gowdy's batting average for the 1913 season was .600. He came to the plate five times and got three hits.

◆ Muddy Ruel, who hit the pop-up that Hank Gowdy dropped, got his nickname because as a boy he liked to play in the mud. Ruel was the catcher when Cleveland shortstop Ray Chapman was hit in the head by a pitch in 1920 and died. It was the only on-field fatality in major-league history.

Also in 1924 . . .

♦ The Giants third baseman Fred Lindstrom, 18, became the youngest player to play in a World Series. Fifty-two years later, he would be in the Hall of Fame.

♦ Wheaties—the Breakfast of Champions—was introduced.

CHAPTER
7

Hack Wilson:
Out in the Sun Too Long

THE DATE: Saturday, October 12, 1929.
THE PLACE: Shibe Park, Philadelphia.
THE SITUATION: Game 4 of the World
Series between the Chicago Cubs
and the Philadelphia Athletics.
Bottom of the seventh.

Hack (George Brace)

FEAT C

ERIES C

ackmen U

ats McCa

efore 30,

N ONE

Root, Nehf

Used Be

re Retire

BLE DE

d Dykes E

Frame—P

ne More G

REBINGE

cw York T

A, Pa., Oc

a toy ham

amite tod

plosion tha

tinent that

ad discovered

he seventh

' McCarthy

laas's Fly

Wilson.

PEECHLESS

house at Los

Team Still

nined.

REBINGER.

m Page One.

l off its pedest

high fly to de

Hack Wilson, C

led about and ra

short, stubby lo

t a blur as th

he ground. He g

time to make t

came down

g sun. Hack lo

ball almost stru

t his feet, and

Boley and Bish

ver the plate a

eted the circuit

It's easy to catch 'em when you're posing for the photographer. But Hack muffed two fly balls in one inning, and the Athletics scored ten runs. (NBL)

scored three runs a

were now only one r

king feeling must ha

Cubs, and as for the f

al rooters from Chicag

assed out long ago. F

was not ended yet,

to gain momentum w

*I*N FOOTBALL AND BASKETBALL, when one team has a huge lead over its opponent, the game is often called a blowout. In baseball, it's usually called a laugher.

The Chicago Cubs had a good laugher going against the Philadelphia Athletics. By the sixth inning, they had built up what seemed to be an insurmountable 8–0 lead. After having lost the first two games of the World Series and winning Game 3, it looked for all the world as though the Cubs were about to tie it all up at two games apiece. President Herbert Hoover was in attendance, watching the humiliation.

Even Connie Mack, the manager of the A's, realized the game was out of reach. He was on the verge of pulling out all his regulars to give his reserve players a chance to play in a World Series. He decided to wait one more inning.

It was a wise move. That inning turned out to be the greatest comeback in World Series history.

IT WAS THE BOTTOM OF THE SEVENTH and right-hander Charlie Root was on the mound for the Cubs. Root (who would become famous three years later for throwing Babe Ruth's "called shot" home run) was working on a three-hitter.

Al Simmons led off for the A's. Simmons had led the

American League with 157 RBIs during the regular season and would become a member of the Baseball Hall of Fame years later. He gave an idea of what was to follow by slamming a home run over the left-field pavilion roof.

It was a nice shot, but nobody in the stands or in the dugouts thought it made much difference, because the Cubs had such a big lead. The hometown crowd applauded politely. At least the A's weren't going to be shut out, they said.

Another future Hall of Famer, Jimmie Foxx, was up next. He singled sharply to right field. Bing Miller stepped up to the plate next and hit a short fly to center field. The Cubs center fielder Hack Wilson lost the ball in the sun and it dropped in for a single. Foxx stopped at second. The hitting parade continued when Jimmy Dykes slapped a single to left and Foxx crossed the plate. It was now 8–2 and two runners were on base. Still, Philadelphia fans weren't getting too worked up over it.

At that point, Connie Mack sensed that Root was losing his stuff and instructed his hitters to start swinging at the first pitch if it was near the plate. That's what Joe Boley did, singling to right field for the fifth consecutive Philadelphia hit. Another run came home.

The Cubs finally got an out when George Burns popped up to short. But it was only a momentary break in the hitting frenzy. The next batter, Max Bishop, bounced a single up the middle and drove in *another* run.

Now it was 8–4, and things were getting interesting. The Cubs' lead didn't seem so big anymore. Cubs fans were beginning to squirm in their seats. The manager, Joe McCarthy, waved frantically for his bullpen to crank up. He came out to the mound to get Charlie Root out of the game before any more damage could be done.

Out of the bullpen came 15-year veteran Art Nehf. McCarthy wanted a lefty to face the next hitter, left-handed center fielder Mule Haas.

There were two men on base when Haas connected with a liner to straightaway center.

FREEZE THIS MOMENT. It was a moment that would be remembered for years by many people, most of all by Cubs center fielder Lewis Robert Wilson. Or, as he was more commonly known, Hack.

Hack Wilson was a funny-looking figure. "He looked like a sawed off Babe Ruth," wrote baseball historian Lee Allen. Hack was only five feet six inches tall, but he weighed 200 pounds and all of it was muscle. He was a power hitter, slamming 39 home runs and 156 RBIs in the regular season. He could hit for average too—.345 that year. A New York newspaper had held a contest specifically to come up with a nickname for him, and the winning entry was Hackenschmidt, after a famous British wrestler of the day. Hackenschmidt became Hack.

Okay, unfreeze that moment. Having already flubbed one fly ball earlier in the inning, Hack was determined not to let this one get by him. Mule Haas hit the ball well, but it was certainly catchable.

Hack moved in at first, then realized he had misjudged the ball and ran back. It was a bright, sunny day, and he was fighting to see. He got under the ball in time to make the catch, but lost sight of it at the last instant. The ball came down and nearly hit him in the head. A gasp came out of the crowd.

Both runners scored easily, and by the time Hack was able to find the ball and throw it in, Haas had torn around the bases for an inside-the-park home run. The score was 8–7 and the hometown crowd was going crazy.

"The A's yelled and danced on their bench like a band of wild Comanches," wrote sportswriter Fred Lieb. Soon they were warbling a popular song of the day—"Sonny Boy"—in honor of Hack Wilson losing the ball in the sun.

Hack, the Cubs, and their fans sank into a cloud of doom. If the Cubs had a laugher going at the beginning of the inning, it sure wasn't very funny anymore.

THE A'S *STILL* WEREN'T FINISHED. Mickey Cochrane (yes, *another* Hall of Famer) was up next. Cochrane was probably disappointed that he was only able to work out a base on balls. When Cochrane walked, Cubs manager Joe McCarthy decided that he'd seen enough of Art Nehf. He brought in right-hander Sheriff Blake.

Al Simmons, who had led off the inning with a homer, was up again. With a 3–1 count, he bounced what looked like a perfect double-play ball to third. As bad luck would have it, the ball took a weird hop and leaped over Bub McMillan's head. Jimmy Foxx followed with his second single of the inning, this time to center, and two more runners scored.

Incredibly, the A's had tied it up at 8–8. And there was *still* only one out.

The crowd, as you can imagine, was in an uproar. "A great gathering of staid Philadelphians had suddenly gone completely out of their minds," wrote John Drebinger in *The New York Times*.

Once again, McCarthy went to the mound in hopes that one of his pitchers might be able to put out the fire. He brought in Pat Malone, the fourth Chicago pitcher of the inning.

Malone proceeded to plunk Bing Miller in the ribs, which loaded the bases. Jimmy Dykes then delivered the final blow of what was the highest scoring inning in World Series history. He sliced a low liner toward the left-field corner. Riggs Stephenson made a dive for the ball near the wall, but it glanced off his glove for a double. Simmons and Foxx scored to make it 10–8.

They didn't have electronic scoreboards in those days. Instead, a "scoreboard boy" would hang a number on a board after each inning. Teams rarely scored ten runs in a single inning, and the scoreboard boy didn't have a board with the number 10 on it. He frantically got a can of white paint and a piece of wood to make one.

Mercifully, Malone struck out Joe Boley and George Burns to end the inning. Fifteen A's had been to bat in what came to be called the Mack Attack. Ten of them got hits. Three of the A's—Simmons, Foxx, and Dykes—got two hits in the inning. It was a spectacular rally.

Connie Mack brought in Lefty Grove to finish up the job for the A's. The Cubs, probably in a state of shock, went down weakly in the eighth and ninth. The final score—Athletics 10, Cubs 8.

"IT WASN'T A BALL GAME," one observer noted. "It was a rodeo."

"Never had a team been more confident of victory than the Cubs as yesterday's game rolled into the seventh inning," commented *The New York Times.* "Never had a team been more annihilated and confounded."

After that crushing defeat, the Cubs were behind three games to one, and the A's were clearly in the driver's seat. The following day the Cubs blew it again, taking a 2–0 lead into the ninth inning and losing the game by a score of 3–2. The Philadelphia Athletics were the World Champions.

The man who led all hitters on both teams with a .471 average for the World Series—Hack Wilson. But what most people remembered was the way he stumbled around the outfield, misjudging two fly balls in that disastrous seventh inning. When he muffed the second one, most agreed, it was the final nail in the Cubs' coffin.

What Happened Afterward

HACK WAS HEARTBROKEN over his errors and refused to speak to the press after the game. Later, he commented, "The sun shining from in back of home plate was blinding. I couldn't see the ball at all after it left Haas' bat until it was almost to the ground. But I should have had that ball, sun or no sun."

When several of his teammates dropped into his hotel room the next morning to console him, the squat outfielder said, "You fellows just cut that out and get out of here. I'm no good and have lost you fellows thousands of dollars. The Cubs ought to send me to a Class B League next year."

As it turned out, the next year Hack had his best year and perhaps the best year *anybody* ever had. He drove in an astounding 190 runs. Nobody has ever driven in more in a single season. He hit 56 home runs, which beat the National League record by 13 and is still the National League record today. His batting average was a hefty .356.

Hack was a good outfielder, but after the 1929 World Series, he couldn't shake his reputation as a bumbler in the field. "He never lived down the Series," said teammate Waite Hoyt.

Hack's playing ability declined rapidly after 1930, mostly because of his fondness for alcohol. He died penniless in Baltimore at the age of 48, three months after Babe Ruth passed away. The National League contributed $350 to pay for his funeral. In 1979, Hack Wilson was inducted into the Baseball Hall of Fame.

Lifetime Statistics

HACK WILSON: Years 12, games 1,348, batting average .307, fielding average .965, home runs 244, RBIs 1,062.

Did You Know . . .

◆ Ten World Series records were set or tied this day:

1. Most hits, one club, one inning (10).

2. Most runs, one club, one inning (10).

3. Most men at bat, one club, one inning (15).

4. Most batters up twice in one inning (6).

5. Most times the same pinch hitter came up in one inning (2).

6. Most home runs, one club, one inning (2).

7. Most runs, both clubs, one game (18).

8. Most base hits by one player in one inning (2).

9. Most total bases, one player, one inning (5).

10. Most runs, one player, one inning (2).

◆ No National League player has ever topped the 56 home runs Hack Wilson hit in 1930. The closest was Ralph Kiner, who slugged 54 in 1949.

◆ On July 1, 1925, Hack hit two home runs in one inning.

◆ Hack hit two home runs in a game 27 times in his career.

◆ Hack, Babe Ruth, and Jimmie Foxx were the only three men in baseball history to hit 50 home runs or more and drive in 150 runs in a season.

◆ Hack's 1930 season was so spectacular, he had more RBIs (190) than games played (155).

♦ Hack had five straight seasons in which he hit .300 or better.

♦ Hack hit 30 or more doubles six times.

♦ Hack led all big league outfielders in putouts in 1927.

Also in 1929 . . .

♦ The Indians and the Yankees became the first major league teams to put numbers on their uniforms.

♦ Cincinnati radio announcer Harry Hartman coined the famous baseball phrase, "Going . . . going . . . gone!"

CHAPTER
8

Umpire Goats

▲ *Don Denkinger (NBL)*
▼ *Cardinals manager Whitey Herzog (NBL)*

Cardinals pitcher Todd Worrell explains to umpire Don Denkinger that when a runner steps on this thing called a base after the ball has already arrived, the runner should be called out. Denkinger saw things differently. The runner (Jorge Orta) scored and the Kansas City Royals went on to win the World Series. (UPI/Bettmann)

MIZE AND RIZZUTO HIT 'BAD' DECISIONS

Other Yankees Also Criti
Umpiring—Call on S
in the Tenth Is Cite

*B*ASEBALL GOATS are not always players. On at least two occasions, they have been *umpires*.

When a ballplayer muffs a fly ball or makes an incredibly stupid baserunning blunder, it's obvious. Everybody can see it. But when an umpire blows a call, it's usually not so blatant.

▲ *Art Passarella (NBL/UPI)*

▶ *Get a pair of glasses, ump! The first baseman is Gil Hodges, taking the throw from Jackie Robinson. Yankees base runner Johnny Sain is obviously safe, but umpire Art Passarella called him out. The next season Passarella was out too—out of a job. (AP/Wide World Photos)*

If it weren't for photography, there would *never* be any umpire goats—because there would never be any proof they had missed a call. But first-base umpire Art Passarella made a whopper on October 5, 1952, and it was captured on film.

IT HAPPENED AT YANKEE STADIUM in the tenth inning of the fifth game of the World Series between the Yankees and the Dodgers. Johnny Sain was the leadoff batter for the Yanks. He sliced a grounder to second. Jackie Robinson scooped the ball up, bobbled it momentarily, and hurriedly threw to first. The Dodgers first baseman, Gil Hodges, stretched as far as he could to gather in the throw. It was a close play, and Art Passarella called Sain out.

The Yankees jumped all over Passarella after the play, hooting and hollering that the runner had been safe. But umpires rarely reverse a decision—especially during the World Series—and Passarella wasn't about to change his mind.

Unfortunately for Art Passarella, an Associated Press photographer happened to click his shutter at the instant Sain stepped on first base. The photo showed Sain's body crossing the base, and his left foot was clearly in the middle of the bag. The photo also showed the ball—it was in midair, at least a foot from Hodges's glove. It was conclusive proof that Sain had beaten the ball to first and the umpire had blown the call.

The Dodgers scored a run in the eleventh inning to win the game 6–5 and take a 3–2 lead in the Series.

"Did you ever see such umpiring?" complained

shortstop Phil Rizzuto (who would later become the Yankees' longtime announcer). "Jiminy cripes! Where do they get them like that? The umpiring in this Series has been terrible."

"You don't mind losing the game," said first baseman Johnny Mize, "but you hate to have it taken away from you that way."

"I don't remember who the umpire was," Johnny Sain said later. "But I do remember that he didn't umpire afterwards."

Sain was right. The Associated Press photo of the play appeared nine inches wide in newspapers the next day. Baseball Commissioner Ford Frick said publicly that umpire Passarella had blown the call. The next season Passarella was out of baseball.

PASSARELLA HAD IT EASY. Back in those days, there were no instant replays to show the world a controversial play over and over again. In fact, television was in its infancy in 1952, and many homes didn't even have a TV.

Thirty-three years later, American League umpire Don Denkinger had it much tougher when he blew a call at a crucial moment in the 1985 World Series. This time, millions of fans in the United States and around the world got the chance to see an umpire make a total fool of himself—from every camera angle, in slow motion, freeze-frame, and even backward.

It was October 26, 1985, at Royals Stadium in Kansas City. The Cardinals were leading the Series by three games to two, and they had a 1–0 lead going into the bottom of the ninth inning of Game 6. Three more outs and St. Louis would be World Champions.

Things were looking good for the Cards. In regular season games in which they had a ninth-inning lead, their record was 84–0. On the mound, they had hard-throwing right-hander Todd Worrell. In Game 5, he had pitched to six hitters and struck out every single one. That tied a World Series record.

Kansas City sent up Jorge Orta to pinch-hit. Worrell got two strikes on Orta, and then the lefty bounced a ground ball wide of first. First baseman Jack Clark picked it up and flipped it to Worrell, who raced over and stepped on the base.

FREEZE THIS MOMENT. First base umpire Don Denkinger, without any hesitation, threw out his arms to signal that the runner was safe. It was obvious to just about anybody watching that Orta was actually out by a good margin. Worrell had beaten him to the bag. But Denkinger said Orta was safe, so safe he was.

The Cardinals, led by manager Whitey Herzog,

went *berserk*. Herzog burst out of the dugout as if he was running from a burning building. He was screaming words that you've undoubtedly heard but shouldn't be printed here, if anywhere.

The television audience around the world watched the instant replay repeatedly. Orta's foot was clearly at least six inches from the bag when Worrell stepped on it. But baseball doesn't use instant replay to make calls, and the decision stood.

WHEN EVERYBODY FINALLY CALMED DOWN, Steve Balboni stepped up to the plate for the Royals. The tying run was on first, the winning run at the plate. On the first pitch, Balboni blooped a high foul pop-up near the Royals dugout. Jack Clark drifted over, and seemed unsure of how much room he had to make the play. The ball plopped harmlessly on the second step of the dugout.

His at-bat saved, Balboni slammed a low, outside fastball in the hole on the left side of the infield for a single. Orta advanced to second.

Men on first and second, nobody out. The tying run was in scoring position. It was a sacrifice situation.

Jim Sundberg dropped a bunt down on the third base side of the mound, but Worrell pounced on it like a cat and threw to third for the force out. There were still runners at first and second, now with one out. Two more outs and St. Louis would win the Series.

But then the roof fell in on the Cardinals. Hal McRae was up as a pinch hitter. Worrell's second pitch to him was a slider that slid too much. Catcher Darrell Porter couldn't hold the ball in his glove, and the runners advanced to second and third. It was ruled a passed ball. The tying run was 90 feet from home plate.

St. Louis elected to intentionally walk McRae in order to load the bases, set up a force play at any base, and possibly get out of the inning on a double play.

Pinch hitter Dane Iorg had other ideas. A lifetime .276 hitter, Iorg was an unsung Mr. October. In 23 postseason at-bats, he collected 12 hits, which works out to a superhuman .522 batting average.

"That's a situation you dream about as a Little Leaguer," Iorg said after the game. "All my life I've dreamed about hitting with the bases loaded in the ninth inning with a chance to win the game."

The left-handed Iorg took ball one inside from Worrell, and then swung at another inside fastball. It wasn't pretty, but the ball looped off the bat and dropped softly in front of right fielder Cesar Cedeno. The tying run came home, followed by Sundberg, who made a spectacular head-first slide around Porter's tag.

The World Series was even at three games apiece. It was an amazing comeback.

AFTER THE GAME, when Cardinals manager Whitey Herzog had time to collect his thoughts, he whined and complained like a baby whose candy had been taken away. "I think it's a disgrace," he said. "You want my opinion? It stinks."

"He knows he blew it," Herzog said of Denkinger, "and millions of people know he blew it. Maybe we shouldn't even show up for Game Seven. We've got about as much chance of winning as a monkey."

Herzog was right. His Cardinals self-destructed the next day, losing 11–0. The rout was marked by temper tantrums, ejections, and fights. At one point, Herzog ran on the field and screamed at Denkinger, "We shouldn't even be out here tonight. We should be home celebrating."

The Cardinals blamed their World Series loss on Don Denkinger, ignoring the pop foul that Jack Clark dropped and Darrell Porter's passed ball. It was all Denkinger's fault, even though the Cardinals hit an anemic .185 as a team, the lowest average ever in a seven-game World Series. They scored just 13 runs in 7 games. (Don't bother getting your calculator. It comes out to 1.85 runs per game.) They had a 3–1 lead in games and blew it.

A deejay in St. Louis announced Denkinger's address and phone number over the air, so fans could bother the umpire during the off-season.

What Happened Afterward

TIMES CHANGE. Instead of being drummed out of baseball like Art Passarella, Don Denkinger continued to be an umpire in good standing after his blown call. Maybe players, fans, and the baseball establishment had come to appreciate that good umpires still make mistakes.

The National Football League began using instant replays to help officials decide close calls in the late 1980s. Some fans complained that using instant replays slowed down games and undermined the authority of the officials. In 1992, the NFL abandoned the practice.

Did You Know . . .

◆ Kansas City's left fielder in the 1985 World Series was Lonnie Smith, who would be the goat of the World Series six years later (see Chapter 11).

◆ In the early days of baseball, one umpire watched the whole field. Runners would take advantage of this, sometimes going from first base to third base without touching second.

◆ Umpires always wear black underwear when they're

on the field—in case they split their pants.

◆ There are six umpires in the Hall of Fame: Al Barlick, Jocko Conlan, Thomas Connolly, Billy Evans, Cal Hubbard, and Bill Klem.

Also in 1952 . . .

◆ Fred Hutchinson of the Detroit Tigers became the last pitcher to serve as a player/manager.

◆ Satchel Paige, at age 47 and perhaps even older, shut out the Detroit Tigers 1–0 in 12 innings for the St. Louis Browns.

◆ Peanuts Lowrey of the St. Louis Cardinals got seven straight pinch hits.

Also in 1985 . . .

◆ Pete Rose got his 4,192nd hit, more than any man in baseball history.

◆ Cal Ripken played his 5,342nd consecutive inning, setting a major league record.

◆ Don Sutton became the first pitcher to strike out 100 or more batters in 20 consecutive seasons.

◆ Tom Seaver won his three hundredth game.

◆ Dale Berra became the second player in major league history to be managed by his father (Yogi). The first was Connie Mack's son Earle.

◆ Cincinnati auto dealer Marge Schott became the owner of the Cincinnati Reds.

CHAPTER
9

Herb Washington:
Designated Pick-off Victim

THE DATE: Sunday, October 13, 1974.
THE PLACE: Dodger Stadium, Los Angeles.
THE SITUATION: Game 2 of the World
Series between the Los Angeles Dodgers
and the Oakland Athletics. Top of the ninth
inning. Runner on first. Nobody out.
Dodgers leading 3–2.

He could run, all right. . . . (AP/Wide World Photos)

1, Col. 7
for the

es, his-
ber the
e 1974
teacher
happing.
date for

class — a class in pickoff
philosophy. Herb has world-
class speed, but it's a different thing running the
bases."

There were two dramatic
high spots for the Dodgers,
the champions of the National
League, outside of Sutton's

two runs padded the Los Angeles lead to 3-0, and the
Dodgers needed all the pad-
ding they had when Oakland
rallied with two runs in the
ninth.

That's when the second
dramatic peak was reached.
Sal Bando led off for the A's,

ing run at the plate, but Los
Angeles had Marshall in the
bull pen. And without further
delay, Manager Walter Al-
ston excused Sutton and
waved for his pitching machine.

Marshall responded on the
gallop, declining a ride from

base
but
dash

M
ingt
and
was
run
seco

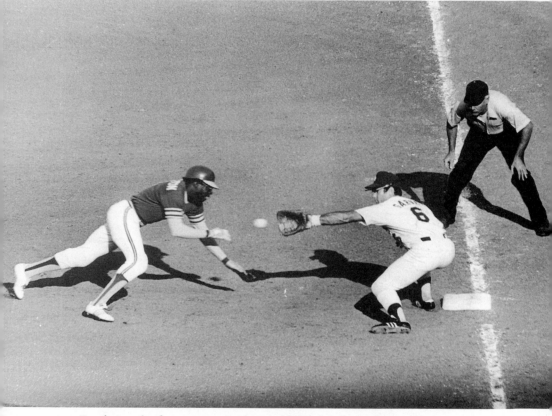

*But being the fastest man in the world didn't help Herb Washington
avoid getting picked off and humiliated. That's Steve Garvey taking
the throw from Dodgers pitcher Mike Marshall. (AP/Wide World Photos)*

$\mathcal{S}$OME GUYS JUST AREN'T CUT OUT to play baseball. You can coach them, train them, show them films,
and surround them with the best players in the world.
They just don't get it. Herb Washington was one of those
guys. Somehow, he managed to get signed by the Oakland Athletics. I'll tell you how in a minute.

AFTER LOSING GAME 1 of the World Series to Oakland, the Los Angeles Dodgers were cruising along with
a 3–0 lead going into the ninth inning of Game 2. Don
Sutton was looking untouchable. And then things began
unraveling.

Sutton tried to get the ball in on Sal Bando, the
leadoff batter, but hit him on the arm. Man on first. The
next hitter, Reggie Jackson, was badly fooled with a
pitch, but Jackson's check swing made contact somehow
and the ball bounced down the third-base line for a
double.

Suddenly the game was interesting—Oakland had
men on second and third with nobody out, and the tying
run was at the plate.

Dodgers manager Walter Alston walked slowly out
to the mound and raised his right arm, the signal for
right-hander Mike Marshall to come in from the bullpen.
Alston had given that signal 109 times that season, an
astounding number of games for one pitcher. Marshall

won 15 of those 110 games (while losing 12) and posted a solid 2.42 earned run average. Marshall was once described as baseball's "perpetual motion pitching machine." He galloped in from the bullpen on foot rather than accept a free ride on the electric cart.

The first batter Marshall faced was Joe Rudi, who hit .293 during the regular season with 22 home runs. Rudi lined Marshall's second pitch into center for a single. Bando and Jackson scored, and the Dodgers' lead was cut to one run. Fans could sense there was a big rally brewing, even after Marshall struck out Gene Tenace for the first out of the ninth inning.

THAT'S WHEN OAKLAND MANAGER Alvin Dark wheeled out 24-year-old Herb Washington from Belzoni, Mississippi. He was the secret weapon of the Oakland A's.

Washington wasn't just any old pinch runner. He was the fastest man in the world. He held the world indoor record for the 50-yard dash (5.0 seconds) and the 60-yard dash (5.8 seconds). Oakland A's owner Charlie Finley had added Washington to the team's roster as a "designated runner," figuring the fastest man in the world would be able to steal lots of bases. The Baltimore Colts football team was also interested in him.

"This will add an element of excitement to the

game," claimed Finley, "and I estimate he will be good for ten wins."

The only problem was that Washington barely knew how to *play* baseball. He had to learn as he went along—in the majors.

If you can run around a track, you can run around a diamond, right? The only difference is that when you're running around a track, nobody's trying to *stop* you. Alvin Dark taught Washington how to run the bases, but the young speed demon still had trouble getting signals from the third base coach and was prone to boneheaded baserunning blunders. On at least one occasion, he made a head-first slide into second base on a hit when he should have rounded the bag standing up and gone all the way to third. Dark admitted that Washington had "no baseball instincts," but felt he could still help the team.

"There is no measuring the effect he had when he got on base," Dark said. "The opposition automatically got jumpy, and you could feel the tension build."

The tension was building in Dodger Stadium when six-foot, 170-pound Herb Washington stepped out of the Oakland dugout to pinch-run for Joe Rudi. It was obvious why Washington was in the game. It was the ninth inning and Oakland needed one run to tie it up. A runner on first needs a double or better to bring him home, but

a runner on second can score on a single. Washington's job was to steal second base, and everybody in the ballpark knew it.

Mike Marshall, the Dodgers pitcher, was no dumb jock. He had a graduate degree from Michigan State University. He also had one of the best pick-off moves in the majors. He had studied the play, dissected it, and perfected it.

Coincidentally, Herb Washington was *also* a graduate of Michigan State. In fact, four years earlier when Washington was a freshman, he took a class in child growth and development. The teacher of the class— Mike Marshall.

The time had come for another lesson.

WASHINGTON TOOK HIS LEAD off first base. He represented the tying run. Manager Dark gave him the sign to steal (in case there were any doubts). Marshall looked in at pinch hitter Angel Mangual, and then stepped off the pitching rubber. Washington moved back to first base.

Marshall looked to the plate again, and Washington opened up another lead. Marshall threw the ball over to first baseman Steve Garvey, but softly. The throw was just a warning. A calling card. Marshall wanted Washington to know he had an eye on him, but he didn't want to show the speedster his best move. They were playing a little game out there.

Washington took a lead once more, a little larger this time, to tease the pitcher.

FREEZE THIS MOMENT. Marshall stepped off the rubber. As Washington casually walked back to first base, Marshall whipped a throw to Garvey. Washington dove for the bag, but it was too late. Garvey had the ball almost as soon as Washington left his feet.

Even the people in the upper deck could see that Washington was out, as 55,989 Dodger fans burst into guffaws. The fastest man in the world had been picked off and humiliated. Washington, who represented the tying run for the A's, walked back to the dugout with his head down. Marshall then struck out Mangual to end the game. The Series was even at one game each.

What Happened Afterward

NEWSPAPERS AROUND THE COUNTRY took delight in seeing the fastest man in the world get faked out of his boots. *The Philadelphia Inquirer* dubbed Washington Hurry-Up Herbie. Its caption below a photo of the pick-off play read: "Washington Sleeps Here."

During and after the season, several members of the

A's told reporters they resented that Washington was taking up a spot on the roster simply because he could run fast. "This will cost someone who should be in the majors a job," complained first baseman Gene Tenace. The always outspoken Reggie Jackson said, "He has as much business playing baseball as I have running the hundred-yard dash." Several of the A's muttered that Washington wasn't ready for the pressure of playing in the World Series.

But Herb Washington couldn't have hurt Oakland too much. They came back to take Games 3, 4, and 5 and win their third consecutive World Series.

A MONTH AFTER THE WORLD SERIES, Herb Washington signed a professional contract to run with the International Track Association. He still found the time to play 13 games for the A's the next season, but after stealing just two bases he never played another game of major league baseball. So far, no other teams have experimented with a designated runner.

If you look up Herb Washington in *The Baseball Encyclopedia*, you'll see the curious statistic that he participated in more than one hundred major league games but never came to bat once and never played an inning in the field.

Lifetime Statistics

HERB WASHINGTON: Years 2, games 104, at-bats 0, batting average .000, fielding average .000, home runs 0, stolen bases 30, runs scored 33.

Did You Know . . .

◆ The designated runner was only one of many innovations Oakland A's owner Charlie Finley tried to introduce to baseball. He also experimented with Day-Glo orange baseballs, three-ball walks, multicolor uniforms, and a 20-second clock between pitches to speed up the game.

To attract fans to the ballpark, he held greased pig chases before the games and wacky promotions such as Bald-headed Men's Day. There was a flock of sheep beyond the right-field fence in the Oakland stadium. The team mascot was a mule, and his name was Charlie O. For the umpires, Finley had air tubes installed to dust off home plate automatically and a mechanical rabbit who brought out fresh baseballs in his paws.

Charlie Finley was also a big supporter of the designated-hitter rule and was one of the main forces that made it part of baseball in 1973.

◆ Bill Buckner, who played left field for the Dodgers in this game, would be the goat of the 1986 World Series (see Chapter 4).

◆ Mike Marshall pitched in all five games of this World Series.

◆ Walter Alston managed the Dodgers from 1954 to 1976. He led them to the World Series seven times. Since Alston retired, Tommy Lasorda has managed the team, so the Dodgers have had just two managers in nearly forty years.

◆ Oakland won the World Series in 1972, 1973, and 1974. No team has won three in a row since, and the only team to do it before was the New York Yankees (1936–39, 1949–53).

Also in 1974 . . .

◆ Hank Aaron belted his 715th career home run, breaking Babe Ruth's lifetime record. The pitcher was Al Downing of the Dodgers.

◆ In an exhibition home-run hitting contest in Tokyo, Aaron defeated Japanese slugger Sadaharu Oh, 10–9.

◆ Horsehide was replaced by cowhide for baseball coverings.

◆ Nolan Ryan became the first pitcher to throw a ball clocked at over 100 miles per hour.

◆ Frank Robinson became the first black major league manager.

◆ Lou Brock broke Maury Wills's single season stolen base record, with 118.

CHAPTER
10

Curt Flood:
It Must Be
Up There Somewhere

THE DATE: Thursday, October 10, 1968.
THE PLACE: Busch Stadium, St. Louis.
THE SITUATION: Game 7 of the World Series between the Detroit Tigers and the St. Louis Cardinals. Seventh inning, two on, two out, no score.

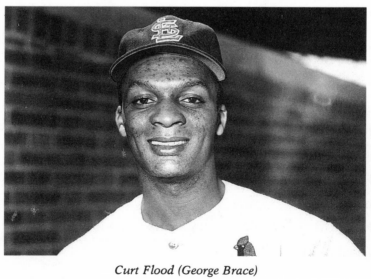

Curt Flood (George Brace)

rs Beat Cards
n World Series

Curt Flood Lets Out of the Bag

Continued from 1st Sports Page

Flood explain his awful blunder and fee sorrier for him than they did for themselv

'Without trying to make any excuses Maxvill said, "everybody in the National L fly balls in the daytin ble. Lou's had trouble ark, I play perhaps 10 f n I do at night," left f much tougher picking

been playing too shall ting on the table, a cig of champagne in his le me off the bat I though er it got up in the air, ball was. I started in . was over my head, I s .... "He looked up at t tors and added, withou t amounts to, I messed g able to see it misju it."

n say to Gibson when asked.

deep breath. "I said . "I said, let's try and

t took another sip of c ewsmen had left him b nd spoke to the few who c we've got a great team vav the last couple of we're still the best te

ught so, too. Like Floo nals, the man who had ies' games was drinkin eat. "We're celebrating good year. Nobody fee es, the better team doe

e disappeared slowly in by bitter sip. Down the walls and players ai hampagne out of bottle

fore they had been do d seemingly out. Denny ission, was "demoraliz d ever come back to S ne was downcast. ["I w ," he told the press want to prove we're a I want it to be Gibson v

vas running around, pow inks on teammates' clc hand, telling had done; Mi ing on a stoo

Mickey Lolich and catcher Bill Freehan of the Tigers, celebrating the World Series victory, thanks to Flood's flub in center field. (NBL/UPI)

STAGE Schoendienst Refuse To Rap Flood's Play

$\mathcal{T}$HE 1968 WORLD SERIES was a real mismatch. On one side were the Detroit Tigers, who hadn't won since 1945. On the other side were the St. Louis Cardinals, World Champions in 1964 and 1967, a team that had won eight of the eleven World Series they had played in. Led by proven stars such as Lou Brock, Curt Flood, Roger Maris, Orlando Cepeda, and Tim McCarver, the Cards were favored to repeat as World Series champions.

But the Tigers put up a good fight. They were down three games to one, but came from behind in the eighth inning to win Game 5, and put together an incredible ten-run inning to win Game 6. The Series came down to one, final seventh game.

AND WHAT A MISMATCH *that* was! The Cards had the best pitcher in baseball on the mound, flame-throwing future Hall of Famer Bob Gibson. All Gibson had done in the regular season was win 22 games and post a 1.12 earned run average—the lowest single season ERA in baseball history. During Game 1 of the World Series, Gibson had thrown a complete game, five-hit shutout and struck out 17 batters. In Game 4, he threw another complete game, five-hitter and hit a home run to top it off. He had won his last seven World Series games in a row.

To face Gibson, the Tigers put up overweight left-hander Mickey Lolich, pitching on just two days' rest. There hardly seemed any point in the Tigers showing up that day.

Gibson was overpowering through six innings. He retired the first ten batters, gave up an infield hit, and then retired the next ten batters. He was intimidating, as he had been all year.

Mickey Lolich was no slouch either, holding the Cardinals scoreless. They had a few good chances to push a run across the plate, but Lolich always seemed to find a way to get an out when he needed one. In the sixth inning, he calmly picked two runners off first base after they had singled—speedster Lou Brock and Curt Flood.

It was Flood who would make a more significant flub in the next inning, a play that would lose the whole Series for the Cardinals.

The game was scoreless. Gibson got the first two hitters out, striking out Mickey Stanley and getting Al Kaline on a grounder to third. But then Norm Cash slashed a single to right field, and Willie Horton bounced a ball through the hole on the left side of the infield for another single. Suddenly, there were two men on base.

Catcher Tim McCarver (now a popular announcer)

trotted out to the mound to chat with Gibson about how he should pitch to the next batter, Jim Northrup. Northrup had hit a grand slam home run just the day before, and the Cards wanted to be particularly careful with him.

Whatever their strategy was, they didn't have much opportunity to implement it. Northrup swung at the first pitch, a fastball on the outside corner, and connected with a drive to center field. The ball was hit hard, but looked playable.

FREEZE THIS MOMENT. Playing center was Curt Flood, probably the best defensive outfielder in the game at the time. Flood was an 11-year veteran who had won a National League Gold Glove Award every year from 1963 through 1968. He once played 226 consecutive games without making an error. Even his initials—C. F.—suggested that he was born to play center field.

It was a sunny afternoon—*too* sunny. It didn't appear that Flood picked up the ball at the crack of Northrup's bat. He might have lost it in all the white shirts behind home plate. He took a step or two forward at first, then realized the ball had been hit harder than he thought, and he slammed on the brakes. The grass was wet from rain two days earlier, and Flood slipped when he tried to change directions.

He started running back, but slipped again and nearly fell, arms flailing as he struggled to get his footing. The ball went over his head and bounced behind him. He finally caught up with it near the wall.

With two outs, Cash and Horton had been running on the pitch. Both scored easily. Detroit 2, St. Louis 0. Northrup flew around the bases and was standing on third by the time the ball got to the infield. Because Flood never touched the ball, the play was ruled a triple, not an error.

The crowd at Busch Stadium fell into stunned silence. Cardinals fans weren't used to seeing their players get picked off bases or misjudge easy fly balls.

Bill Freehan was the next hitter for Detroit, and he lined a double into the gap in left. Northrup scored, making it 3–0. The Tigers got another run on three singles in the ninth.

The Cards got a run in the bottom of the ninth on a Mike Shannon home run, but it was—as they say in baseball talk—too little, too late. Final score: Detroit 4, St. Louis 1. What should have been a third out turned into a World Series–winning two-run triple.

Mickey Lolich, who won three complete game

victories in the World Series, had actually outpitched the great Bob Gibson. The lowly Tigers had actually outplayed the St. Louis Cardinals. Detroit became only the third team ever to come back from a 3–1 deficit and win the World Series. (The first two were the 1925 Pirates and 1958 Yankees.)

"WORLD SERIES GOATS, move over," wrote *The Philadelphia Inquirer* the next day. "Make room for Curtis Charles Flood."

"I feel sorry for him, so sorry for him," said teammate Orlando Cepeda. "What can you say to him, a guy who plays there for years, who never makes mistakes?"

"All it amounts to," admitted Flood glumly, "is that I messed it up. I might have been playing too shallow. After it got up in the air, I didn't know where the ball was. I don't mess up balls like that too often. It will probably go down in the annals of baseball history."

What Happened Afterward

UNLIKE THE OTHER PLAYERS in this book, Curt Flood will *not* be remembered for the rest of his life because of an error he made in a single baseball game. A year later, Flood was traded to the Philadelphia

Phillies and he shocked the baseball establishment by refusing to go. For eighty years, baseball had operated under a system in which players were bound for life to their original team unless they were traded, sold, or released. Flood contended that baseball teams should *not* have the right to pass around men like they were used cars. The player should be able to determine his own destiny.

Curt Flood brought a lawsuit against Baseball Commissioner Bowie Kuhn, the presidents of the American and National Leagues, and all the team owners. He took his case all the way to the Supreme Court. In the end the justices ruled against him, but his effort paved the way for the free agency system, which began three years later.

Today, free agents who sign multimillion-dollar contracts owe a debt of gratitude to Curt Flood. *That's* what he'll be remembered for.

Flood came back to play for the Washington Senators in 1971, but only hit .200. He retired from baseball before he could be a free agent himself, so he never enjoyed the rewards of his struggle. After his baseball career, he went on to become a guitar teacher, cartoonist, sportscaster, and commissioner of Little League baseball in Oakland, California.

Lifetime Statistics

CURT FLOOD: Years 15, games 1,759, batting average .293, fielding average .987, home runs 85.

Did You Know . . .

♦ When Roger Maris popped up to shortstop for the third out of the seventh inning, it was the final at-bat in his memorable career.

♦ In 1966, Flood handled the ball 396 times without a

*Gold Glove winner Curt Flood on a better day,
making a spectacular catch. (NBL)*

single error. Between the 1965 and 1966 seasons, he went 226 games before making an error.

Five times during his career, Flood got five hits in a game. On August 16, 1964, he got eight hits in one *day*. He came to bat nine times during the doubleheader and came away with five singles, two doubles, and a triple.

The same season, Flood got eight hits in eight consecutive at-bats. The record is 12, set by Pinky Higgins of Boston in 1938.

On June 19, 1967, Flood made an unassisted double play. That happens fairly often among infielders, but Flood played center field!

Also in 1968 . . .

Denny McLain won 31 games, becoming the first pitcher to win 30 or more since Dizzy Dean did it in 1934. Nobody has done it since.

Don Drysdale set a major league record by pitching 58 consecutive scoreless innings. Drysdale's mark was broken by Orel Hershiser in 1988.

Washington Senators shortstop Ron Hansen made an unassisted triple play.

Catfish Hunter pitched a perfect game, and he also got three hits and drove in four runs.

Detroit Tiger Jim Northrup hit three grand-slam home runs in five days.

CHAPTER
11

Lonnie Smith:
Faked Out of
the World Series

THE DATE: Sunday, October 27, 1991.
THE PLACE: The Metrodome, Minneapolis, Minnesota.
THE SITUATION: Game 7 of the World Series between the Atlanta Braves and the Minnesota Twins. Top of the eighth inning. No score. Runner on first. Nobody out.

Lonnie Smith (The Atlanta Braves)

*With heavy-hitting Terry Pendleton (.319) following him in the
Atlanta lineup, Lonnie Smith had plenty of opportunity for base-
running adventures. Here he is crashing into Twins catcher
Brian Harper in Game 4. Harper held on to the ball and
Smith was called out. (AP/Wide World Photos)*

aves Have a Huge Edge:
e Lonnie Smith Factor

*L*ONNIE SMITH always had a knack for being in the right place at the right time. He came up to the big leagues as a rookie with the Philadelphia Phillies in 1980, and the Phils won the World Series that year. In 1982 Smith was playing for the St. Louis Cardinals, and *they* won the World Series. In 1985, he was with the Kansas City Royals, and *they* went all the way too.

When Smith joined the last-place Atlanta Braves and they won the National League pennant in 1991, he became the first man to play in four World Series with four different teams.

"I'm just blessed," said Smith. "I just happened to be in the right place at the right time."

With "the Smith Factor" on their side, it seemed like a sure thing that Atlanta would win the 1991 World Series. They would have, too, if Lonnie Smith hadn't been in the *wrong* place at the *wrong* time.

THE SERIES WAS ALL TIED UP at three games apiece in one of the most exciting Fall Classics ever. When Lonnie Smith came to bat leading off the eighth inning of Game 7, he had already hit three home runs in three consecutive games. In this game, he'd had a walk and a bunt single. The game was scoreless. Jack Morris was pitching a gem for the Twins.

On a 1–0 pitch, Lonnie took a half swing and blooped

a soft single into right field. The potential World Series–winning run was on base. Terry Pendleton, the National League's leading hitter and Most Valuable Player, was up.

Smith danced off first base, and Jack Morris kept a close watch on him. Smith had been nicknamed Skates because of his tendency to fall down in the field and on the bases, but he could steal a base or two. One season he swiped 68 of them. Morris threw over to first three times between the first two pitches to Pendleton.

With a 1–2 count, Smith took off for second. Pendleton swung at the outside fastball and rammed a long drive in the gap in left center-field.

FREEZE THIS MOMENT. Most of the time, a runner on first base will score on a double. In fact, a *turtle* with a cast on its leg should be able to score from first on a double.

Unfortunately, Lonnie Smith got faked out of his shoes by the decoy of the century. A decoy occurs when a player in the field *pretends* to make a play for the purpose of fooling a base runner. As soon as the ball was hit, rookie second baseman Chuck Knoblauch went through the motion of picking up a ground ball. He "tossed" this imaginary ball to shortstop Greg Gagne, who was near second base. It's an old trick meant to make the base runner think he is being forced out at second. Hardly anybody ever falls for it, at least not in the big leagues.

But Lonnie Smith did. He was halfway to second base when he heard the crack of Pendleton's bat. At that instant, he should have looked to see where the ball was headed so that he would know what to do next:

♦ If the batted ball was a grounder, he should have slid into second.

♦ If it was a fly that might be caught, he should have headed back to first.

♦ If it was a single, he should have continued running past second and stopped at third.

♦ If it was an extra-base hit, he should have turned on all the jets and come around to score.

Smith's crucial mistake was that he didn't look to see where the ball was going. When he saw Knoblauch and Gagne go into their little pantomime, he assumed the ball had been hit on the ground and he immediately slowed down.

Meanwhile, the ball had bounced off the warning track and hit the wall. Smith suddenly realized he'd been fooled, but he didn't know where the ball was. He rounded second and came to a dead stop. He peered into the outfield.

Instead of standing there looking like Columbus searching for sight of land, Smith should have been looking at his third-base coach, Jimmy Williams. When he finally saw Minnesota center fielder Kirby Puckett pick up the ball, Smith hurried to third base.

"That was terrible!" proclaimed announcer Jack Buck as Lonnie Smith pulled into third base and Pendleton into second.

EVEN WITH SMITH'S MISTAKE, Atlanta still had runners on second and third with nobody out. The Braves had the opportunity to break the game wide open and win the Series. The Twins nervously moved their infield in, hoping to stop a run at the plate.

But the Braves couldn't score. Ron Gant bounced out weakly to first and the runners were forced to hold. David Justice was walked intentionally to load the bases, and Sid Bream grounded into an inning-ending double play. Lonnie Smith was a force-out victim at home plate.

The score stayed at 0–0 until the bottom of the tenth, when Minnesota pushed across a run on a bases-loaded single. That gave them the ballgame and the Series. If Lonnie Smith hadn't stopped running in the eighth inning, the Braves would have been the World Champions.

What Happened Afterward

"SMITH PULLED A BASERUNNING ERROR that should put him right up there with Fred Merkle in baseball's bonehead department," announced *The Sporting News*. "The Braves lost because Lonnie Smith stood transfixed at second base," wrote *USA Today*, which headlined a story about the game, LONNIE'S BOGUS JOURNEY TRIPS BRAVES.

The big question was, why did Lonnie stop at second base? If he fell for the grounder decoy, why didn't he slide? Maybe he didn't fall for the decoy at all—maybe he simply didn't know where the ball was. Maybe he forgot that the object of the game is to score runs.

Smith wouldn't talk to reporters after the game. "We got Lonnie's attention," Minnesota shortstop Greg Gagne told reporters. "He got all confused out there, and it was the big play of the game."

"He didn't run. He held up," said perplexed Atlanta manager Bobby Cox. "Why? I don't know. I don't know what he was thinking. Ask Lonnie."

A few days later, Lonnie Smith admitted he had been faked out. "If I saw Pendleton's ball off the bat, there's a good chance I could have scored," he said. "But I didn't look in. That was my mistake."

———

IN RECENT YEARS, when somebody makes a monumental blunder like Lonnie Smith did, the newspapers call up the goats of World Series past to comment on it.

"Tell Lonnie that it's just a baseball game," said Bill Buckner, who let a dribbling grounder go through his legs to lose the 1986 World Series for the Boston Red Sox (see Chapter 4). "I just think it's not right to pick out one particular play. I think it was more important that the guys behind Lonnie didn't get him in."

"Lonnie will be all right," said 75-year-old Mickey Owen, whose passed ball blew the Brooklyn Dodgers' chances in 1941 (see Chapter 3). "Nine out of ten runners would've done the same thing."

Lifetime Statistics (through 1992)

LONNIE SMITH: Years 15, games 1,475, batting average .289, fielding average .964, home runs 90, stolen bases 360.

Did You Know . . .

♦ The home-plate umpire for this game was Don Denkinger, who blew a call and became the goat of the 1985 World Series (see Chapter 8).

◆ The 1991 World Series was a first in many ways: It was the first to have four games decided on the last pitch. It was the first to have five games decided in a team's last turn at bat. It was the first to have three extra-inning games. It was the first to have a seventh game go scoreless through nine innings. It was the first to have two teams that had gone from last place to first place in a single season.

◆ In 1982, Lonnie Smith led the National League in runs with 120.

◆ In winning this game, the Minnesota Twins extended their streak to eight consecutive World Series game victories in the Metrodome. They have never lost a Series game there.

◆ Twins second baseman Chuck Knoblauch, who pulled the decoy on veteran Lonnie Smith, won the American League Rookie of the Year award in 1991.

Also in 1991 . . .

◆ Otis Nixon of the Atlanta Braves stole six bases in one game, setting a modern National League record.

◆ Forty-four-year-old Nolan Ryan pitched his seventh no-hitter. The same night, Rickey Henderson stole his 939th base, breaking Lou Brock's career record.

◆ Dennis Martinez of the Expos pitched a perfect game

against the Dodgers. It was the fifteenth perfect game in baseball history.

♦ The directors of the Baseball Hall of Fame ruled that no one on baseball's ineligible list can be on the ballot for election. This took Pete Rose out of Hall of Fame contention.

♦ The National League awarded franchises to Denver and Miami. The Rockies and the Marlins begin playing in 1993.

♦ David Cone of the Mets struck out 19 men in a game against the Phillies, tying a National League record.

CHAPTER
12

Babe Herman: Rush Hour on the Basepaths

THE DATE: Sunday, August 15, 1926.

THE PLACE: Ebbets Field, Brooklyn, New York.

THE SITUATION: Midseason game between the Brooklyn Dodgers and the Boston Braves. Bottom of the seventh inning. Tie score.

Floyd Caves "Babe" Herman (NBL)

The clown prince of the Brooklyn Dodgers. Babe was known to trot in from the outfield when there were only two outs, and legend has it he was bonked on the head by a fly ball he was trying to catch. (NBL)

TO DOUBLE PLAY!

*T*HE BLOOPERS, BLUNDERS, AND BONEHEAD PLAYS described in this book, for the most part, were crucial ones. Fred Merkle's baserunning blunder blew the pennant for the 1908 Giants. Mickey Owen, Bill Buckner, Lonnie Smith, and the others made plays that cost their teams the World Series.

This chapter concerns a mistake that *didn't* lose a World Series. It didn't lose a pennant either. It didn't even lose a *game*. In face, this play *won* the game.

However, over the years and decades since it happened, the story of Babe Herman tripling into a double play has become a legendary example of the classic baseball screwup. It has been passed down from generation to gencration— baseball's equivalent to George Washington chopping down the cherry tree. And once again, the man who got the blame for making such a colossal mistake wasn't really at fault.

The Brooklyn Dodgers were one of the worst teams in baseball in the 1920s and 1930s. They earned a reputation for being clowns and buffoons who couldn't run, hit, throw, or field, but they seemed to have a good time on and off the diamond. These lovable losers were referred to as the Daffiness Boys.

During spring training of 1926, a six foot four inch, big-eared, buck-toothed, 22-year-old rookie named Floyd Caves Herman reported to the Dodgers training camp. Caves was his *actual* middle name, not his nickname. Herman's nickname was Babe, because he was a left-handed power hitter who reminded people of Babe Ruth.

It wouldn't be long before Babe Herman established himself as the clown prince of the Dodgers—the biggest buffoon of them all. Babe was known for trotting in from the outfield when there were only two outs in the inning. He would talk to a reporter, suddenly pull a cigar out of his pocket that was already lit, and act as if nothing was unusual about that.

Baseball historians will probably argue for centuries whether Babe was once bonked on the head by a fly ball he was trying to catch. Sportswriter John Lardner wrote, "Floyd Caves Herman did not *always* catch fly balls on the top of his head, but he could do it in a pinch."

It would take a whole book to fully describe Babe's misadventures in the outfield and on the basepaths, but one play in particular gives him his place in history— probably the strangest double play ever made.

IT WAS THE BOTTOM of the seventh inning of a game between the Dodgers and Boston Braves. The score was tied at 1–1. Babe was at the plate with one out and the bases loaded—Chick Fewster on first, Dazzy Vance on second, and Hank DeBerry on third. The names of the base runners are only mentioned here because they become important as soon as the ball leaves Babe's bat.

Left-hander George Mogridge was on the mound for the Braves. He tried to get a curveball by Herman, but it hung and Babe jumped all over it, slamming a drive off the right-field wall that was just a few feet from being a home run. It looked like a sure double or maybe even a triple.

That's when the fun began.

FREEZE THIS MOMENT. All four Dodgers took off with the crack of the bat. DeBerry, who was on third, trotted home to score easily. That put the Dodgers in the lead, 2–1.

Dazzy Vance, the runner on second, stopped halfway to third because he wasn't sure if the ball would be caught. When he saw it hit the wall four hundred feet from home plate, he dashed to third. Vance was never a fast runner, so he rounded the bag and stopped there.

Chick Fewster, who had been on first base, reached second easily and could have made it to third. But as he rounded the second base bag, he saw Vance was standing on third. Fewster realized that he couldn't get to third if his teammate was already on the base, so he pulled up and stopped at second.

Babe Herman, meanwhile, had his head down and

legs churning as he motored around the diamond. Babe figured, logically enough, that his blast off the wall would clear the bases. He could practically smell the RBIs he was piling up.

When Fewster turned around and saw Herman barreling toward second base, he figured he had better get out of there, and fast. Fewster took off for third.

By that time, the Braves had picked up the bouncing ball and rifled it toward the infield.

Seeing the ball coming in, Dazzy Vance decided he had no chance to reach home plate, so he stood on third despite the fact that he saw a traffic jam coming upon him. Fewster steamed into third base. Babe Herman, hot on his heels, slid into third as well.

The Dodgers had three runners jockeying for position to keep a foot on third base. It looked like rush hour at Grand Central Station.

The umpire, Charley Moran, scratched his head. So did the Dodgers third-base coach Mickey O'Neil.

The Braves second baseman Doc Gautreau took the relay from right fielder Jimmy Welsh and rifled it to third base. The third baseman, Andy High, looked at the scene before him. He scratched his head too.

"Babe," umpire Moran said to Herman, "you're out for passing Fewster on the baseline." Herman realized the ump was right and walked off the field.

"Well, I guess I'm out too," said Fewster. He headed out to right field for the next inning.

Gautreau, the second baseman, grabbed the ball from Andy High and followed Fewster.

"Chick, look what I got," Gautreau said, and tagged Fewster with the ball.

"Fewster, you're out!" shouted umpire Moran.

"I thought I was out five minutes ago!" complained Fewster.

"Ha, ha, I'm safe," said Vance, still standing on the bag.

He would have been safe, too. Unfortunately, with Herman and Fewster both tagged out, the inning was over.

LIKE MANY OF THE STORIES in this book, the man who was labeled a goat for life wasn't really to blame. In this case, it was really third-base coach Mickey O'Neil's fault for allowing Dazzy Vance to stand on third while the ball was rattling around in right field. Babe Herman would be remembered for the rest of his life as the first and last man in baseball history to triple into a double play. (Some say he tripled into a *triple* play, but there was one out when he hit the ball.) Not many people even recall that the Dodgers won the game, and that Herman's hit drove in the winning run.

For years after this play took place, whenever somebody mentioned that the Dodgers had three men on base, somebody was sure to reply, "Oh, yeah, which base?"

What Happened Afterward

AFTER FINISHING THAT ROOKIE SEASON with a .319 batting average, Babe Herman developed into one of the most feared hitters in the game. In 1929 he hit an astonishing .381. The next season he even managed to top it, hitting .393. That year he collected 241 hits, 35 homers, and 135 RBIs. (Oddly enough, he didn't win the batting title either year. Lefty O'Doul hit .398 in 1929 and Bill Terry hit .401 in 1930.) Although he led National League outfielders in errors for three straight seasons, he became more than competent defensively after a few years in the majors.

Herman played for Cincinnati, Chicago, Pittsburgh, and Detroit before finishing his 13-year career with a lifetime average of .324. He would probably be enshrined in Cooperstown today, if he hadn't become famous for catching fly balls with his head or sharing third base with two of his teammates. Babe Herman died in 1987 in Glendale, California.

Lifetime Statistics

BABE HERMAN: Years 13, games 1,552, batting average .324, fielding average .971, home runs 181, stolen bases 94, RBIs 997.

*A rare photo of two legendary goats—
Babe Herman and Hack Wilson. (NBL)*

Did You Know . . .

Babe slammed the first home run ever hit by a major league player in a night game. It happened in Cincinnati on July 10, 1935.

On July 20, 1933, Babe Herman hit three home runs and drove in eight runs in one game. The record for RBIs in one game is 12, set by Jim Bottomley in 1924.

Babe hit into three double plays in one game against the Phillies in 1936. The record is four, set by Joe Torre in 1975.

Babe got nine hits in nine consecutive at-bats over the course of two games in 1926.

In 1929, the entire Brooklyn outfield hit over .300. Babe hit .381, Rube Bressler hit .318, and Johnny Frederick hit .308.

During World War II, when many major leaguers were in the service, the 42-year-old Babe came out of retirement to lend a hand to his old team, the Brooklyn Dodgers. He had been out of the game for eight years, but played 37 games and hit .265.

After his career was finally over, Babe made his living by scouting young players for the Pirates (1946–50), the Yankees (1953–54), the Phillies (1955–59), the Mets (1961), the Yankees again (1962–63), and the Giants (1964).

Also in 1926 . . .

◆ Babe Ruth hit three home runs in Game 4 of the World Series.

◆ Grover Cleveland Alexander, 39, came out of the bull-pen in Game 7 to strike out Tony Lazzeri and save the World Series for the Cardinals.

◆ Firpo Marberry saved 22 games for Washington, setting a major league record.

◆ Dutch Levsen became the last pitcher to win two complete games in one day.

◆ The St. Louis Browns and the New York Yankees played the shortest game in American League history—55 minutes.

◆ Mel Ott, at 17, became the youngest National League player to get a pinch hit.

Want To Read More About These Stories?

About Fred Merkle:
The Unforgettable Season by G. H. Fleming (Holt, Rinehart and Winston, 1981).

About Merkle, Fred Snodgrass,
Heinie Zimmerman, and Hank Gowdy:
The Giants of the Polo Grounds by Noel Hynd (Doubleday, 1988).

About Mickey Owen:
Baseball in '41 by Robert Creamer (Viking, 1991).

About Bill Buckner:
The Curse of the Bambino by Dan Shaughnessy (Dutton, 1990)
One Strike Away: The Story of the Red Sox by Dan Shaughnessy (Beaufort Books, 1987).

About Hack Wilson:
Hack by Robert S. Boone and Gerald Grunska (Highland Press, 1978).

About Herb Washington:
Charlie O. and the Angry A's by Bill Libby (Doubleday, 1975).

About Babe Herman:
The Brooklyn Dodgers: An Illustrated Tribute by Donald Honig (St. Martin's Press, 1981).

About all the World Series stories:
The World Series: A 75th Anniversary, edited by Joseph L. Reichler (Simon & Schuster, 1978).
The History of the World Series by Gene Schoor (William Morrow & Co., 1990).
The Story of the World Series by Fred Lieb (Putnam, 1949).
World Series: The Games and the Players by Robert Smith (Doubleday, 1967).
The World Series by Lee Allen (Putnam, 1969).

Also, it's fun to look up old issues of newspapers to see how these events were reported at the time. Ask in the microfilm department of your library.

Index

PLAYERS AND PEOPLE

Aaron, Hank, 121
Aguilera, Rick, 54–56
Alexander, Grover Cleveland, 152
Allen, Lee, 92
Alston, Walter, 114, 121

Backman, Wally, 55
Baird, George, 17
Balboni, Steve, 107
Bando, Sal, 114–15
Barlick, Al, 111
Barnes, Virgil, 80
Barrett, Marty, 54
Baylor, Don, 66
Bentley, Jack, 81, 84
Benton, Rube, 71–75
Berra, Dale, 111
Berra, Yogi, 111
Bishop, Max, 92
Blake, Sheriff, 94
Boggs, Wade, 54, 61, 66
Boley, Joe, 91, 95
Bonham, Tiny, 43
Boyd, Oil Can, 55
Bream, Sid, 137
Bresnahan, Roger, 5, 17
Bressler, Rube, 151
Bridwell, Al, 7, 12
Brock, Lou, 121, 124–25, 140
Buck, Jack, 137

Buckner, Bill, *x*, *xi*, 48–65, 120, 139, 144
Burns, George, 91, 95

Carter, Gary, 56–57, 66
Casey, Hugh, 39–45
Cash, Norm, 125–27
Cedeno, Cesar, 108
Cepeda, Orlando, 124, 128
Chase, Hal, 76
Cicotte, Eddie, 75
Clark, Jack, 106–7, 109
Clemens, Roger, 52–53
Cobb, Ty, 33
Cochrane, Mickey, 38, 47, 94
Collins, Eddie, 71–75
Cone, David, 141
Conlan, Jocko, 111
Connolly, Thomas, 111
Coolidge, Calvin, 84
Coscarart, Pete, 38
Costas, Bob, 55, 59
Cox, Bobby, 138
Craig, Roger, 66

Dark, Alvin, 115–17
Darling, Ron, 65
Davis, George, 86
Dean, Dizzy, 131
DeBerry, Hank, 145–46
Denkinger, Don, 105–10, 139
Devlin, Art, 5–6
Devore, Josh, 22–23, 30

Dickey, Bill, 43
DiMaggio, Joe, 37, 42–47
Donlin, Mike, 5
Downing, Al, 121
Doyle, Larry, 23
Drebinger, John, 94
Drysdale, Don, 131
Durocher, Leo, 38–39, 42
Dykes, Jimmy, 91, 94–95

Emslie, Bob, 7, 12
Engle, Clyde, 26–29
Evans, Billy, 111
Evers, Johnny, 5–11, 17

Faber, Urban, 71
Felsch, Happy, 71–72, 74, 75
Fewster, Chick, 145–48
Finley, Charlie, 115–16, 120
Fischer, Bill, 57
Fletcher, Arthur, 24
Flood, Curt, 122–30
Foxx, Jimmie, 91, 94, 95, 98
Frazee, Harry, 50
Frederick, Johnny, 151
Freehan, Bill, 127
French, Larry, 38
Frick, Ford, 105
Frisch, Frank, 82
Fullerton, Hugh, 30

Gagne, Greg, 66, 135–36,
   138
Gandil, Chick, 74, 75
Gant, Ron, 137
Gardner, Larry, 30
Garvey, Steve, 117–18
Gautreau, Doc, 147–48

Gedman, Rich, 59
Gehrig, Lou, 47
Gibson, Bob, 124–28
Goetz, Larry, 40
Gordon, Joe, 43
Gowdy, Hank, 77, 78–86
Grove, Lefty, 95

Haas, Mule, 92–93, 96
Hansen, Ron, 131
Harrelson, Bud, 57–59
Harris, Bucky, 81
Hartman, Harry, 99
Henderson, Dave, 54
Henderson, Rickey, 140
Henrich, Tommy, 39–45
Henriksen, Olaf, 24
Herman, Babe, 142–51
Hernandez, Keith, 55, 66
Hershiser, Orel, 131
Herzog, Buck, 5
Herzog, Whitey, 106–7, 109
Higgins, Pinky, 131
High, Andy, 147–48
Hodges, Gil, 104
Hofman, Solly, 9
Holke, Walter, 71, 74–75
Hooper, Harry, 22–23, 27–28
Hoover, Herbert, 90
Horton, Willie, 125–27
Hoyt, Waite, 97
Hubbard, Cal, 111
Hughes, Tom, 86
Hunter, Catfish, 131
Hurst, Bruce, 56
Hutchinson, Fred, 111

Iorg, Dane, 108

Jackson, Michael, 63
Jackson, Reggie, 114–15, 119
Jackson, Shoeless Joe, 71–77
Jackson, Travis, 83
Johnson, Davey, 53, 56
Johnson, Walter, 81–84
Joss, Addie, 17
Justice, David, 137

Kaline, Al, 125
Kauff, Benny, 76
Keller, Charlie "King Kong,"
    42–43
Kiner, Ralph, 98
Klem, Bill, 15, 74, 111
Knight, Ray, 57–59, 61, 66
Knoblauch, Chuck, 135–36,
    140
Kroh, Floyd, 10
Kuhn, Bowie, 129

La Guardia, Fiorello, 37
Lardner, John, 145
Lasorda, Tommy, 121
Lazzeri, Tony, 152
Leibold, Nemo, 81
Levsen, Dutch, 152
Lewis, Duffy, 22, 29
Lieb, Fred, 30, 93
Lindstrom, Fred, 81, 84, 86
Lolich, Mickey, 125–27
Lopez, Nancy, 66
Lowrey, Peanuts, 111

Mack, Connie, 80, 90, 91, 95,
    111
Mack, Earle, 111
Malone, Pat, 94

Mangual, Angel, 117–18
Mantle, Mickey, 47
Mantle, Mutt, 47
Marberry, Firpo, 152
Maris, Roger, 124, 130
Marquard, Rube, 17, 21, 33
Marshall, Mike, 114–18, 121
Martinez, Dennis, 140
Mathewson, Christy, 4, 10–12,
    17, 21–33, 85
Mathewson, Henry, 33
Mazzilli, Lee, 53
McCarthy, Joe, 92, 94
McCarver, Tim, 124–25
McCormick, Moose, 6–7, 8, 11
McGinnity, Joe, 9–10, 17
McGraw, John, 4, 11, 15, 16,
    21–22, 29–31, 75, 80, 85
McLain, Denny, 131
McMillan, Bub, 94
McMullin, Fred, 75
McNamara, John, 53, 63
McNeely, Earl, 84
McRae, Hal, 108
Medwick, Ducky, 44
Merkle, Fred, *x*, 2–17, 21,
    25, 31, 36, 62, 75, 85, 138,
    144
Meusel, Irish, 84
Meyers, Chief, 25, 28, 31
Miller, Bing, 91, 94
Miller, Ralph, 82
Mitchell, Kevin, 56–57, 59, 66
Mize, Johnny, 105
Mogridge, George, 146
Moran, Charley, 147–48
Morris, Jack, 134–35
Murphy, "Grandma," 43

Murray, Red, 22, 24–25, 27
Myers, Hy, 39

Nehf, Art, 92–94
Niekro, Phil, 66
Nixon, Otis, 140
Northrup, Jim, 126–27, 131

O'Day, Hank, 9, 11
O'Doul, Lefty, 149
Oh, Sadaharu, 121
Ojeda, Bob, 52–53
O'Neil, Mickey, 147–48
Orta, Jorge, 106–7
Ott, Mel, 152
Owen, Mickey, 34–47, 62, 139, 144

Paige, Satchel, 111
Passarella, Art, 103–5, 110
Pendleton, Terry, 135–38
Pfiester, Jack, 4–7, 12
Porter, Darrell, 108–9
Puckett, Kirby, 137
Pulliam, Harry, 12–13, 15

Rariden, Bill, 72–73
Reese, Pee Wee, 43
Reiser, Pete, 38–39, 43
Ripken, Cal, 111
Risberg, Swede, 75, 77
Ritter, Lawrence, 27
Rizzuto, Phil, 105
Robertson, Dave, 71, 75
Robinson, Bill, 60
Robinson, Frank, 121
Robinson, Jackie, 104

Robinson, Wilbert, 30
Rolfe, Red, 39
Root, Charlie, 90–92
Rose, Pete, 66, 111, 141
Rudi, Joe, 115–16
Ruel, Muddy, 81–84
Ruth, Babe, 50–51, 90, 97, 98, 121, 145, 151
Ryan, Nolan, 121, 140

Sain, Johnny, 104–5
Schiraldi, Calvin, 55–56
Schott, Marge, 111
Seaver, Tom, 111
Sergio, Michael, 65
Seymour, Cy, 5
Shannon, Mike, 127
Simmons, Al, 90–91, 94–95
Smith, Lonnie, 110, 132–40, 144
Snodgrass, Fred, 18–33, 36, 62, 75, 85
Speaker, Tris, 22–25, 28–29, 33
Stahl, Jake, 23–24
Stanley, Bob, 57–61
Stanley, Mickey, 125
Stapleton, Dave, 63
Steinfeldt, Harry, 5
Stephenson, Riggs, 95
Sturm, Johnny, 39
Sundberg, Jim, 107–8
Sutton, Don, 66, 111, 114

Tenace, Gene, 115, 119
Tenney, Fred, 4, 14
Terry, Bill, 149
Thompson, Homer, 33
Thompson, Tommy, 33

Tinker, Joe, 5–10, 17
Toney, Fred, 77
Torre, Joe, 151

Vance, Dazzy, 145–48
Vaughan, Arky, 47
Vaughn, Hippo, 77

Wagner, Heinie, 24
Walker, Dixie, 38, 43
Walsh, Ed, 17
Wasdell, Jim, 38, 43
Washington, Herb, 112–21
Weaver, Buck, 75
Welsh, Jimmy, 147
Williams, Jimmy, 137
Williams, Lefty, 76
Williams, Ted, 47
Wills, Maury, 121
Wilson, Hack, 88–99
Wilson, Mookie, 57–60, 63, 66
Wood, Smokey, Joe, 22–25
Worrell, Todd, 106–8

Yerkes, Steve, 28–30

Zimmerman, Heinie, 68–77, 85

TEAMS
Atlanta Braves, 132–40
Boston Braves, 77, 80, 86, 142–51
Boston Red Sox, 18–33, 48–66, 139
Brooklyn Dodgers, 34–47, 50, 104, 139, 142–51
California Angels, 64, 66

Chicago Cubs, 2–17, 77, 88–99, 149
Chicago White Sox, 68–77
Cincinnati Reds, 77, 86, 111, 149
Cleveland Indians, 66, 99
Detroit Tigers, 13, 111, 122–31, 149
Kansas City Royals, 62, 106–10, 134
Los Angeles Dodgers, 46, 112–21, 141
Minnesota Twins, 66, 132–40
Montreal Expos, 140
New York Giants, 2–17, 18–33, 47, 50, 68–77, 78–87, 144
New York Mets, 47, 48–66, 141, 151
New York Yankees, 34–47, 50, 99, 104–5, 121, 128, 152
Oakland Athletics, 112–21
Philadelphia Athletics, 80, 88–99
Philadelphia Phillies, 128–29, 134, 141, 151
Pittsburgh Pirates, 4, 8, 128, 149, 151
San Francisco Giants, 151
St. Louis Browns, 152
St. Louis Cardinals, 37, 38, 106–10, 111, 122–30, 134, 152
Washington Senators, 78–86, 129, 131, 151

BALLPARKS
Busch Stadium, St. Louis, 122–27

Dodger Stadium, Los Angeles, 112–20
Ebbets Field, Brooklyn, 34–47, 142–48
Fenway Park, Boston, 18–30
Griffith Stadium, Washington, 78–84
Metrodome, Minneapolis, 132–40

Polo Grounds, New York, 2–16, 68–75
Royals Stadium, Kansas City, 106–10
Shea Stadium, New York, 48–65
Shibe Park, Philadelphia, 88–96
Tiger Stadium, Detroit, 33